PANDORA'S BOX

PANDORA'S BOX

Feminism Confronts Reproductive Technology

NANCY LUBLIN

ROWMAN & LITTLEFIELD PUBLISHERS, INC.
Lanham • Boulder • New York • Oxford

ROWMAN & LITTLEFIELD PUBLISHERS, INC.

Published in the United States of America
by Rowman & Littlefield Publishers, Inc.
4720 Boston Way, Lanham, Maryland 20706

12 Hid's Copse Road
Cummor Hill, Oxford OX2 9JJ, England

British Library Cataloguing-in-Publication Information Available

Library of Congress Cataloging-in-Publication Data

Lublin, Nancy, 1971–
    Pandora's box : feminism confronts reproductive technology / Nancy
Lublin.
        p.   cm.
    Includes bibliographical references and index.
    ISBN 0-8476-8636-1 (cloth : alk. paper).—ISBN 0-8476-8637-x
(pbk. : alk. paper)
    1. Human reproductive technology—Social aspects.   2. Feminism.
I. Title.
RG133.5.L83   1997
176—dc21   97-26354
                                                                  CIP

ISBN 0-8476-8636-1 (cloth: alk. paper)
ISBN 0-8476-8637-x (pbk.: alk. paper)

Printed in the United States of America

♾ ™ The paper used in this publication meets the minimum requirements of
American National Standards for Information Sciences—Permanence of Paper for
Printed Library Materials, ANSI Z39.48–1984.

To the strong and
beautiful feminists in my life—
Abby, Alix, Barbara, Christy, Eleanor, Fwa, Gerry,
Ivan, Jaq, Kelly, Kimani, Linds, Mary, M.O'S, Ros, and Sheri—
who remind me that diversity is something we can and should celebrate.

Contents

Acknowledgments

*M*any people and institutions provided solace, structure, and Snackwells during the writing and revision of this project.

At Brown University, I was pushed to give intellectual credence to my activist instincts by people like Stephen Graubard, Vartan Gregorian, James Morone, and Darrell West. I am grateful for their patience, scholarship, and sincere commitment to teaching. Marti Rosenberg and the 2:1 Coalition to Preserve Choice were superlative shepherds to Students for Choice and one particularly rambunctious sheep.

The Marshall Aid Commemoration Commission granted me the opportunity to grow in the surreal petri dish that is Oxford, England. G. A. Cohen and Elizabeth Frazer gave me the chance to pursue my interests in feminist theory. Mark Philp was a tremendous supervisor for my final two terms in Oxford. Nicola Lacey knew exactly when to be tough and when to provide a tissue and chocolate. Her insight, suggestions, and example continue to be invaluable. My afternoons with Sheila Kitzinger comprise some of my most cherished memories of Oxford. Elizabeth Frazer and Ann Oakley were helpful, patient, and provocative examiners.

At New York University School of Law, Dean John Sexton was extremely supportive and encouraging. In David Richards, I found a true teacher, philosopher, and comrade. Maryanne Case and Sylvia Law provided very helpful comments and suggestions. Steve Kelban, director of the Root-Tilden-Snow Program, has been a heroic mentor and friend.

I am indebted to Ivan Zimmerman at Planned Parenthood of New York City who read (and reread) drafts with a virtual magnifying glass. He also supported my Snackwells habit. Annie Keating and the staff of NARAL/NY were friends as well as a tremendous resource.

In addition to providing comments, Mary Ann Castle, Dorchen Leidholdt, and Drucilla Cornell are role models whom I admire. They teach feminism by example.

Kannon Shanmugam edited drafts on a regular basis and functioned as my grammatically gifted mentor. Jennifer Ruark, Robin Adler, and the friendly staff at Rowman & Littlefield managed not to giggle at some of my more naive questions. Helen Bequaert (Becky) Holmes read through the manuscript with remarkable care, for which I will be eternally grateful.

Christy Cannon-Lorgen, Rosalind Bark, Catherine Hovaguimian, and Andrew Woodburn were good listeners. Finally, my parents and my best friend, Faith Salie, were patient confidants and pillars of strength. It was during a conversation on the telephone with my mother that the title was conceived, so to speak.

The Institute for Women's Policy Research and Center for Policy Alternatives in Washington, D.C. and the National Abortion and Reproductive Rights Action League generously granted me permission to reprint the charts herein.

Many discussions and experiences with other people inspired the ideas and arguments in these pages. The mistakes are purely my own.

INTRODUCTION

Woman in England pregnant with seven!
Well, Hello Dolly! Sheep Cloned!
Abortion pill approved!
63 year-old woman gives birth!
Comatose pregnant woman kept alive by machines!
Teenage couple delivers baby at home in bathtub!

ecently, these stories captured the front page of newspapers worldwide. There were television movies and magazine articles, talk shows and advice columns. Arnold Schwartznegger found himself pregnant declaring, "My body, my choice!" in the film *Junior,* dinosaurs that were created and altered *in vitro* roamed *Jurassic Park,* and soap operas included story lines on infertility.[1] Simply, we are fascinated by technological intervention in the womb.

Popular sentiment aside, sociologists, anthropologists, historians, medical ethicists, biologists, and psychologists have all remarked upon the wonder of reproduction and the significance of human intervention in the womb. The ability to see, explain, and change human reproduction involves social, political, legal, and ethical questions concerning sexuality, motherhood, and, most of all, power. Not surprising, feminists have also commented a great deal upon the significance of the ability to control fertility, assist conception, intervene during pregnancy, and mediate childbirth.

Is technological intervention the friend or foe of women? This book examines an array of answers to this question, canvassing the paradigms that feminists utilize to respond to technological intervention in the womb. My motivation is to find a feminist language that speaks to women's diverse experiences and preferences. As we face a new century, I seek to outline a feminist framework that is

xi

inclusive of all women. Indeed, this diversity—the reality of women—is my foremost concern.

The Scope of My Inquiry

Although many feminists and organizations successfully specialize in individual reproductive technologies or categories of interventions, there are several important reasons to create comprehensive feminist frameworks with respect to all technological intervention in the womb. Creating a holistic response to contraception, infertility, prenatal technology, and birth within which individual technologies can be discussed will abet feminist activism and theory. Chapter 1 outlines the scope of technological intervention in the womb and gives several reasons for the need of feminist theory and activism to think about reproductive technology in this new way. The remainder of the book seeks to define what these feminist frameworks might include.

Feminism is a myth. The existence of a single theory of political, economic, and social equality or a single definition of women's rights and interests is impossible. Since the sexuality, race, class, age, religion, and singing ability of women vary greatly, so our visions and constructions of the feminist utopia are also multitudinous.[2] Furthermore, there are varying views regarding the nature of causes and agents of oppression, corrective measures, and the integrity of the category "women" itself. Consequently, "feminisms" is a more accurate term.

However, although feminism is a broad category, not every woman with a theory is a feminist. Lamenting the recent trend of hyper-inclusion under the feminist umbrella, bell hooks wrote, "Currently feminism seems to be a term without any clear significance. The 'anything goes' approach to the definition of the term has rendered it practically meaningless."[3] There should be prerequisites to wearing the feminist badge. Although feminisms are diverse, I believe that this kaleidoscope of visions contains core elements.

All feminisms are united in that they identify political dystopias and develop normative arguments concerning justice for women. In

1972, Alison Jaggar provided one of the first taxonomies of the political philosophies of women's liberation. She argued:

> Feminists are united by a belief that the unequal and inferior social status of women is unjust and needs to be changed. But they are deeply divided about what changes are required. The deepest divisions are not differences about strategy or the kinds of tactics that will best serve women's interests; instead, they are differences about what are women's interests, what constitutes women's liberation.[4]

As Laura Purdy contends, core feminism requires two main judgments: (1) women are worse off than men and (2) this state of affairs is unjust and should be remedied.[5] Simply, all feminisms focus upon gender fairness. Distinct feminisms may identify gender inequities in various arenas and shaped by various sources, such as economic disparity or legal discrimination or biology, but these disparate understandings are related in their identification of gender inequality as an actuality and a form of injustice that must be rectified.

Chapters 2 through 5 canvass potential feminist responses to technological intervention in the womb, celebrating the diversity of feminisms in the tradition of earlier taxonomic works by Alison Jaggar and Rosemarie Tong.

Chapter 2 explains the technophilic endorsement of technological intervention in the womb. I cite two particular feminists, Shulamith Firestone and Donna Haraway, who contend that as long as females and males are needed for reproduction, biological sex has reproductive meaning. Firestone argues that reproductively purposeful difference is the source of women's oppression. If reproduction were void of human participation and made a public commodity, she contends that biological difference would be eradicated and sexual equality established. Haraway does not ascribe as much meaning to sexual difference, yet she also argues that feminists ought to embrace technological intervention in the womb. Rather than ectogenic reproduction, Haraway foresees the self-replication of part-organic, part-machine hybrids called "cyborgs" as potentially inspiring a post-gender world.

Chapter 3 is dedicated to technophobia, the fear and disdain for technological intervention in the womb as hostile to women.[6] Similar to Firestone's view of women as a sex-based class, technophobes believe that biological sex is indicative of character and lifestyle; they presume *all* women possess certain attributes. For example, one important essential trait of women is our supposed relationship with nature. So-called "ecofeminism" contends that women are in harmony with the earth, peace, and the natural order. In hopes of improving Mother Nature's design, technological intervention in the womb interferes with women's natural balance. Accordingly, these feminists believe that any artificial invasion of a woman's body is inherently "anti-women" and thus they reject the very idea of technological intervention in the womb.

Chapter 4, "Technophobia: (FINR)RAGE against the Machine," refers to an international organization of women (Feminist International Network of Resistance to Reproductive and Genetic Engineering) that laments the actual administration and allocation of reproductive technology. If technophobic radical feminists deem technological intervention in the womb as *innately* anti-women, FINRRAGE feminists label reproductive technology effectively anti-women. They argue that culture—the values, institutions, and relationships that shape society—is male-dominated. Technological interventions in the womb are administered and developed by particularly male-dominated institutions: science and medicine. Consequently, it is not the idea of all technology, but rather the practice of certain technologies, that FINRRAGE feminists oppose in the name of all women.

Chapter 5 considers the "My body, my right!" response to technological intervention in the womb and explains how the Supreme Court has determined that decisions concerning reproductive technology are protected individual liberties under the rubric of the right to privacy. However, the Supreme Court is not a bastion of core feminist principles. Chapter 5 also presents the feminist understanding of the right to privacy, explaining the differences between what the Supreme Court has decided and what these feminists desire. Revering the sanctity of freedom from government intervention, privacy feminists call for "the extension of the promise of liberalism to women,"[7] stressing the rationality of all individuals and the universal need for human rights. Making technology legal and available to women is a tributary of a larger "keep-government-off-our-backs" scheme in the fight for personal liberty.

Although I seek to demonstrate a matrix of feminisms, I am critical of these feminist frameworks for providing inadequate responses to our most descriptive feature: diversity. These feminisms do not validate the real implications of these technologies and/or the real experiences and differences among women as women.

Catharine MacKinnon once noted, "It is common to say that something is good in theory but not in practice. I always want to say, then it is not such a good theory, is it?"[8] I seek a praxis feminism, a theory that recognizes the reality of women's situation, particularly the differences among women, and creates a transcendent understanding in harmony with this actuality. Praxis means the practice of theory, the performance of understanding. Thus, praxis feminism is the "struggle to unite theory and practice in action and reflect upon the world in order to transform it for women."[9]

Chapter 6 explores several praxis feminisms. Embracing the best elements of other feminisms and also recognizing both women and technology in the context of social reality, materialist feminisms are cognizant of the importance of theory made to match practice. Materialist feminisms, particularly the work of Rosalind Petchesky, Ruth Colker, and Catharine MacKinnon, are extremely praxis-oriented methodologies. This chapter endorses advocacy of the Equal Protection Clause as a potential legal materialist feminist response to technological intervention in the womb.

Consequently, although there exists a plethora of feminisms united by common core principles, I endorse one feminism as the best response to technological intervention in the womb in the name of gender justice. In Chapter 7, I suggest some intuitions regarding the substance of this feminist framework. Also, I will acknowledge that my promotion of materialist feminism and, more specifically, the equality perspective implies assent to particular beliefs about law as a potentially effective mechanism for feminist social change and the state as the agent responsible for resolving gender inequalities.

In demonstrating the importance of an inclusive feminist dialogue about gender justice, I desire the creation of a framework that includes not only all technological intervention in the womb and all women, but the important work of a diaspora of feminist theories. Third-wave feminist scholarship need not be rejectionist or dismissive. We should seek to extract the most insightful elements of earlier feminist work, the lessons of those experiences, so that we can effectively revise the future.[10] It is true that in these pages many theories and theorists are reduced to a few brief sentences and categorized with oversimplicity. There are comprehensive expositions that delve deeper into the intricacies of feminist theory. My intention is to outline the broad contours of a debate and the simple, neat style is intentional; I believe more people (new feminists, young feminists, non-American feminists) should be included in this discussion. Truly, my mission is to excite people about feminist theory and advocacy more generally, with the intention of building a solid feminist framework for discussing and effecting social change.

Notes

1. For example, see 1994–96 story line involving "Maria" and "Edmund" on *All My Children*. Also, in England, see the Summer 1997 story line involving Max and Susanna on *Brookside*.

2. In celebration of this diversity, the anniversary issue of *Ms.* magazine in January 1994 contained a beautiful spread called "The Faces of Feminism," which included pictures and short biographies of more than twenty feminists. Also, see a recently published anthology of third-wave feminists, Barbara Findlen, ed., *Listen Up: Voices from the Next Generation* (Seattle: Seal Press, 1995).

3. bell hooks, "Feminism: A Movement to End Sexist Oppression," in *Feminism and Equality*, Anne Phillips ed. (New York: New York University Press, 1987), 62–76, 68.

4. Alison Jaggar, "Political Philosophies of Women's Liberation," reprinted in *Feminism and Philosophy*, Mary Vetterling-Braggin, Frederick Elliston, and Jane English, eds. (Totowa, N.J.: Rowman and Allanheld, 1977), 5–21, 5.

5. Laura Purdy, *Reproducing Persons: Issues in Feminist Bioethics* (Ithaca: Cornell University Press, 1996), 5–18 (defining core feminism as having two parts). See also Jane Flax, "Women Do Theory," in *Feminist Frameworks*, 3rd ed., Alison Jaggar and Paula Rothenberg eds. (New York: McGraw-Hill, 1993), 80–85 (claiming feminism has three goals: to understand the power differential between men and women, to understand women's oppression, and to effect action in the name of overcoming the oppression).

6. Obviously, the terms technophilia and technophobia refer more generally

to the love and fear of all technology (not just intervention in the womb). Philia and phobia are often utilized to suggest irrational behavior. Moreover, these terms do not necessarily refer to feminists. It is clear at the beginning of chapters 2 and 3 that herein these terms refer only to the rational feminist love, and fear, of technological intervention in the womb.

7. Zillah Eisenstein, *Feminism and Sexual Equality* (New York: Monthly Review Press, 1984).

8. Catharine MacKinnon, "From Practice to Theory, or What Is a White Woman Anyway?" *Yale Journal of Law and Feminism* (1991): 13–22, 13.

> "To be good in theory but not in practice posits a relation between theory and practice that places theory prior to practice, both methodologically and normatively, as if theory is a terrain unto itself. The conventional image of the relation between the two is first theory, then practice. You have an idea, then act on it. In legal academia you theorize, then try to get some practitioner to put it into practice. To be more exact, you read law review articles, then write more law review articles. The closest most legal academics come to practice is teaching their students, most of whom will practice, being regarded by many as an occupational hazard to their theorizing."

Inspired by this very MacKinnon quote, Ruth Colker wrote a short piece for a symposium at Northwestern University Law School called "The Practice of Theory," reprinted in *Northwestern University Law Review* (1993): 1273–285.

9. Maggie Humm, *Dictionary of Feminist Theory*, 2nd ed. (London: Harvester Wheatsheaf, 1995), 218.

10. Susan Faludi, "I'm Not a Feminist, But I Play One on TV," *Ms.* (March/April 1995): 30–39, 32. This article argues that the "new wave" of feminist authors are not revisionist feminists, as they have often been called, but rejectionist feminists. Also lamenting the new wave, Anna Quindlen called this individualist movement "Babe Feminism." See her editorial column, "Public & Private," *New York Times*, 19 January 1994. She wrote, "It's babe feminism—we're young, we're fun and we do what we want in bed—and it has a shorter shelf life than the feminism of sisterhood. I've been a babe, and I've been a sister. Sister lasts longer."

1

DEFINITION AND
JUSTIFICATION

*W*hat is technological intervention in the womb?
Most generally, technological interventions in the womb are extraneous parties (objects or people) that hinder, modify, or enhance female reproduction. I identify four main categories of reproductive technology: contraception, assisted conception, prenatal technology, and birth technology. Although most of this chapter focuses upon anecdotes and examples from the first two categories, my analysis applies to all four types of intervention.

Contraception refers to the prevention of pregnancy. Female fertility-control devices (contraceptive technology) include barrier methods (sponge, diaphragm, and cervical cap), hormonal prescriptions (oral ingestives,[1] Norplant, and Depo-Provera), surgical prevention (intrauterine device, hysterectomy, and sterilization), and post-coital methods (morning-after pill, surgical abortion, and RU 486).[2] The Alan Guttmacher Institute estimates that

> Of the 58 million U.S. women of reproductive age (15–44), 39 million (67%) are at risk of an unintended pregnancy (they are currently sexually active, fertile, and not pregnant or seeking pregnancy). Nine in ten use some contraceptive method; sterilization and the pill are most commonly used followed by the condom, diaphragm and other methods.[3]

Assisted conception, commonly known as "infertility treatment" (though many methods are highly experimental), refers to technol-

1

ogies that help women conceive and become pregnant. In-vitro fertilization, surrogacy, embryo freezing and transfer, egg harvesting and donation, and therapeutic donor insemination (TDI)[4] constitute conceptive technologies and arrangements. It has been estimated that as many as 4.9 million married couples in the United States want to be parents but are unable to conceive.[5]

Prenatal technology refers to interventions during the development stages of pregnancy. These include prenatal surgery, testing, and monitoring. Suturing so that the cervix will hold during pregnancy, an operation referred to as a "purse string," is an example of prenatal surgery. The alpha-fetoprotein test (AFP), chorionic villus sampling (CVS), and fetoscopy are forms of screening. Fetal heart-rate monitoring, contraction stress tests (known as the oxytocin challenge test), and visual technologies such as ultrasound are forms of monitoring.

Finally, *birth technologies* are technological interventions used during childbirth. This category includes medically induced labor through a variety of techniques, episiotomy, Cesarean section, use of forceps, anesthesia, shaving, and both internal and external electronic fetal-monitor devices. In the United States, 99 percent of all births take place in hospitals.[6] In 1991, 23.5 percent of all births were Cesarean deliveries, up from 5.5 percent in 1970.[7]

Specialized Treatment

Feminist theorists and activists often specialize in particular categories of intervention or specific technologies for the following three reasons.

First, these interventive techniques and devices seem to involve separate emotional and physical dilemmas. Attempts to prevent pregnancy are endeavors quite separate from attempts to become pregnant or to monitor and deliver pregnancy in that they appear to implicate disparate medical phenomena. Moreover, even particular types of reproductive technology are dissimilar. Some technologies are extremely invasive while others involve no penetration of the body. Further, some technologies are highly artificial while others rely on more natural techniques. For example, a three-month hormonal injection is, at one level, quite different from inserting a honeycap.

The second reason why many feminist activists and theorists often focus upon a more narrow vision is that they are concerned with political efficacy. Organizing around a particular area or writing about a specific subject—single-issue politics—is often a politically sensible methodology, as it allows greater intimacy with the arguments, players, statistics, and studies, fostering accuracy and impetus. For example, the National Abortion and Reproductive Rights Action League (NARAL) is the largest feminist membership organization in the United States, with over three hundred thousand members. Until 1993, it was focused solely upon making abortion safe, legal, and accessible.[8] Thereafter, it expanded its platform to include all forms of contraception (still a narrow aspect of reproduction and women's liberation). Under the leadership of Kate Michelman, NARAL-national and vibrant state affiliates have influenced local, state, and national politicians through tremendous lobbying and advocacy efforts. With respect to advocacy of woman-centered childbirth, Sheila Kitzinger has published dozens of books relating to midwifery, breast-feeding, and other childbirth topics. Most recently she has focused on waterbirth, organizing the first world conference on the topic in London in 1995. Kitzinger's work as an advocate of woman-centered models of maternity care has touched the lives of women worldwide, as her publications have been translated into more than twenty languages. Consequently, single-issue theory and activism can be quite effective.

However, the most persuasive reason why feminists contemplate reproductive technologies disparately is not the supposed emotional and physical diversity of technologies or concerns about efficacy, but social interpretation. Many feminists believe that issues of motherhood and non-motherhood have different social meaning. Access to contraception means that women's (hetero)sexuality can be free of reproductive meaning. Simply, contraception breaks the link between the concepts "woman" and "mother," and thus women can properly argue that they should not be treated as potential mothers, but as people. Conversely, many feminists, such as Rosalind Petchesky, argue that access to infertility treatments (or some, like Gena Corea, even argue the very existence of such treatments) fosters regressive understandings of women as mothers. They argue that the social meanings of fertility and infertility treatment are not only incompatible, but at odds—one representing liberation from sex-role stereotypes, the other reinforcing claustrophobic roles.

Reasons for Creating a Comprehensive Framework

Although I am deeply grateful for the specialized work of many feminists and the focused activism of various organizations, there is also a need for a grassroots response capacious to technological intervention in the womb. A comprehensive feminist framework can supplement specialized theory and activism for the following reasons:

1. Success in the political arena requires a comprehensive response to technological intervention in the womb.

Massive amounts of money, time, and energy are dedicated to understanding and controlling human reproduction, specifically women's bodies and most notably our wombs. As with the billion-dollar missions to the moon and Mars, or the massive pilgrimages to the Wild Wild West, scientists are anxious to colonize this last frontier. This enterprise is quite controversial. Parallel to the debates that loom over the National Aeronautics and Space Administration (NASA) regarding flight plans, future goals, appropriate costs, and even the value of space exploration itself, technological intervention in the womb is the object of great contention, with various agents involved in the political arena. From religious groups to insurance companies, many special interests hope to influence public policy decisions. Moreover, many of these agents have a comprehensive attitude toward reproductive technologies.

The Catholic Church is a powerful political agent in U.S. policy making. The National Conference of Catholic Bishops and several other well-funded, non-profit organizations lobby government officials, inviting their support for Catholic directives. In addition to these official organizations, individual Catholics exert great influence upon political decision making through the vote and other means of political participation. Furthermore, Catholic individuals and organizations have considerable power over hospital boards and doctors, who administer these commodities.[9]

All present Catholic positions on reproduction can be reduced to two simple principles set out by Pope Paul VI in the famous 1968 encyclical "Humanae Vitae": justice and chastity. The former refers to the manufacture and destruction of the embryo, an entity that according to Catholic doctrine constitutes human life. Any creation of life (namely, infertility treatments) or disposal of life (all post-coital contraception) is deemed immoral. "Through these procedures [in vitro fertilization and voluntary destruction of embryos], life and death are subjected to the decision of man, who thus sets himself up as the giver of life and death by decree."[10] According to this Catholic teaching, post-coital contraception and all forms of assisted conception fail the test of justice,[11] though prenatal technologies and interventions during birth monitor and facilitate human life.

The second principle, chastity, here applies to the Catholic doctrine that conjugal sex should be inseparable from reproduction. The "marital act" has an "inseparable connection of unitive and procreative significance."[12] From this physical union, husband and wife are meant both to experience closeness and to generate new life. Therefore, sexual relations that are not procreative and/or do not involve conjugal love are sinful.[13]

> The sexual activity, in which husband and wife are intimately and chastely united with one another, through which human life is transmitted is 'honorable and good. . . .' The church teaches as absolutely required that in any use whatsoever of marriage there must be no impairment of its natural capacity to procreate human life.[14]

Thus, any use of contraception represents a conscious attempt to have non-generative coitus, a sin according to the chastity principle.

These two principles established, specific technologies may then be evaluated and deemed moral or sinful accordingly. The 1968 text itself begins with the explanation and exposition of basic teachings, followed by individual questions answered in the body and conclusion of the encyclical. Catholic rules are declared, and specific situations and devices are contemplated with these standards in mind.[15] All technology is not necessarily blanketly accepted or rejected, and debate has ensued among various Catholics regarding the application of these principles,[16] but each intervention is contemplated against these same two principles.

Jewish law is not as standardized as Catholic doctrine. Since there are several forms of Judaism (including Orthodox, Conservative, and Reform), no single source of teaching analogous to papal authority exists. However, *Halakhah*, Jewish law, has formed the backbone of all Orthodox and many Conservative Jewish civilizations for centuries. Based upon a combination of four sources—the Bible, Talmud, medieval codes, and commentaries—the *Halakhah* is a subject of much debate, with rival rabbis interpreting it differently. In *Women and Jewish Law*, Rachel Biale explains the history of several *Halicic* debates and teachings with respect to selected women's issues. According to her, two biblical passages appear to be of great influence where *Halicic* directives regarding sexuality and reproduction are concerned.

First, the original man and woman, Adam and Eve, are believed to have embodied natural sexual characteristics that apply to all subsequent women and men: women are passive, receptive, and saddled with the pain of childbirth as punishment for Eve's original sin, while men are aggressive and strong. Simply, Judaism relies upon a strong understanding of difference: men and women are innately different. Consequently, the majority of *Halicic* teachings argue that when God says, "Be fruitful and multiply and fill the Earth and subdue it,"[17] he is speaking only to Adam, since Eve is incapable of filling or conquering anything. Biale argues that most Jewish law suggests that "for men procreation is a positive commandment, but for women it is only an act of choice and free will."[18] The generative facet of sex is important only in accordance with other desired goods such as pleasure, restraining the man from sin,[19] and adherence to the *onah* and *niddah*.[20] Consequently, contraception, sex during pregnancy, and sex with a sterile partner are all permissible.

The second important biblical passage is a story of a man hitting the belly of a pregnant woman, who then miscarries.[21] According to Biale, most *Halakhah* says that if the woman is not harmed but the fetus is, then the aggressor pays a fine to the husband similar to property damage. However, if the woman is harmed, then the aggressor should be charged with a capital crime. Thus, *Halakhah* identifies a difference between the fetus and woman: the fetus is only potential life, a form of property, while the woman is *nefesh*, a living human or "self." (The Talmud explains that the fetus becomes *nefesh* when most of its head is outside the woman's body.[22]) Having noted this definition of *nefesh*, the principle of *pikuah nefesh*, self-preservation, follows: all individuals and communities at large should be concerned with the nourishment of human life. It is this respect for the self-preservation of living human beings, specifically women, that grounds Jewish positions on post-coital contraception, prenatal technologies, and interventions in birth: the self-preservation of the mother should be the foremost concern.

Jewish people debate how to apply the "self-preservation of the mother" standard. All *Halicic* teachings support abortion to save the life of the mother. Some Jews believe that this "life or death" concern is the only appropriate interpretation of self-preservation. However, Jewish law has taken a more generous view, recognizing quality of life as significant. Biale writes: "In 1977 the Israeli Knesset codified prevailing practice by permitting abortion in cases of serious hazard to the mother; conception from adultery, child pregnancy and rape; suspicion of severe birth defects and cognitive disease; and pressing socioeconomic factors that would prevent the parents from providing the essentials of a healthy environment."[23] An agreement between Likud and the right-wing Agudat Yisrael in 1979 as part of the new coalition government repealed the last clause. Most recently, the Orthodox gains in the Knesset may mean further restriction of the grounds for abortion.[24] However, regardless of the debates about application of *Halicic* law, there is agreement upon a framework, basic principles to guide this dialogue.

Biale's book was published in 1984, when infertility technologies were starting to spread to labs worldwide but not yet to the pages of public discourse. Although she did not discuss *Halakhah* with respect to specific conceptive technologies, it is certain that rabbis and scholars debate the justice of these regimens within the confines of Jewish principles outlined by the Bible, Talmud, medieval codes, and commentaries. Simply, new issues and questions are set against the backdrop of old theories and teachings and the appropriate application of these agreed-upon principles.

The purpose of considering the Catholic and Judaic responses to technological intervention in the womb here is not to admire their specific teachings, or even to criticize them from a feminist perspective,[25] though a large body of literature is dedicated to this end. It is not their ideology, but the *method* that invites attention herein. It is important to note that both Catholicism and Judaism endorse an internally consistent, comprehensive understanding of reproduction under the umbrella of larger principles.

Besides the host of religious agents in the political arena, feminists must compete with one of the most organized and well-funded political forces in America, insurance companies. Many reproductive interventions are costly, involve short-term and/or long-term risk, and are controversial in certain communities. Insurance companies are businesses concerned with maximizing profit and limiting liability. Gender justice is only a concern of insurance companies to the extent that they comply with basic non-discrimination laws in this area, unless promoting feminism happens to be a profitable venture. Consequently, their decisions on what to insure, as well as what to lobby for and endorse politically, are driven almost entirely by a single principle—economic greed. The idea that all technological intervention in the womb is subject to this principle is a tautology, since all businesses are driven by the profit motive. Insurance company executives may disagree about how to achieve maximum profits and these decisions may be complex or even wrongly decided. However, insurance companies also have a comprehensive framework to guide their dialogue of assessment of technological intervention in the womb.

If feminists are to compete with these rival political agents, let alone try to find ways to cooperate with or infiltrate them, feminist arguments and platforms should be constructed in a similar fashion. Taking a fragmented approach when rival agents have comprehensive views is equivalent to arranging a chorus of talented singers with no sheet music. Feminists will falter in the political arena in the face of well-prepared foes unless we approach the subject matter in an equally comprehensive, competitive manner.

2. Feminism requires philosophical integrity and consistency.

Present marginalized perceptions of technological intervention in the womb have led to confusion and, at times, vitriolic arguments among people who genuinely care about the same objective, the well-being of women. Fundamental questions regarding when life

8

begins and under what conditions technology is acceptable should be settled before specific technologies can be indicted or endorsed within the social and political context of women in a given society. I am urging proficiency in the same home language, a common framework within which a dialogue can occur. I do not mean to imply that feminists in Thailand should adopt American policies, or that American feminists should adopt the same claims as Chilean feminists. Of course the use of amniocentesis in India and China should be discussed within the context of women's choices and conditions in those specific societies. However, in any place where feminism flourishes it should recognize the importance of a broad vision of justice, a comprehensive umbrella of principles covering all technological interventions in the womb.

Debate within feminism—discussion among people who care about the well-being of women—is not only healthy, but productive. Ruth Colker refers to this as a "good-faith dialogue":

> A good-faith dialogue is one embedded in respect for the people affected by the issue under discussion as well as the arguments made on each side of the issue. Let us assume that two people disagree about the morality of women having abortions. Their discussion might not be good-faith dialogue if, for example, the pro-life advocate did not respect the well-being of women. Alternatively, the discussion might not be in good-faith if the pro-choice advocate did not respect the value of prenatal life. On the other hand, that discussion could be a good-faith dialogue. Why? Because people who respect the well-being of women can consider abortion to be immoral. In addition, people who consider abortion to be moral can respect the value of prenatal life.[26]

Robin Morgan has referred to the need for what she calls a "feminist diplomacy":

> It involves respect, courtesy, risk, curiosity, and patience. It means doing one's homework in advance, being willing to be vulnerable, and attentively listening to one another. (A sense of humor never hurts, either.) Skill improves with practice, and practicing feminist diplomacy is challenging, exhilarating, rewarding—and at times exhausting.[27]

Indeed, there are several notable battles among feminists who specialize in the politics of particular reproductive technologies. Eleanor Smeal, former director of the National Organization for Women and founder of The Feminist Majority, has publicly denounced Janice Raymond's position against RU 486 for undermining pro-choice abortion politics. However, Smeal has not criticized Raymond's extensive work against high-tech solutions to infertility. If "My body, my choice" is the slogan for the abortion rights struggle, doesn't this pro-choice rhetoric apply to infertility technologies as well? When Rhonda Copelon called for a legal right to self-determination, it was in the context of a critique of privacy as the justification for abortion:

> At the center is the question of whether women are entitled to be self-determining, for to be denied control over reproduction or sexuality is to be denied full personhood and reduced to dependence. . . . What we need is recognition of an affirmative right of self-determination, one rooted in equality and social responsibility. This requires not simply the protection of choice, but the provision of the material and social conditions that render choice a more meaningful right rather than a mere privilege.[28]

Does this reproductive self-determination also refer to the right to have a water birth or a home birth, or the right to be a surrogate? Thelma McCormack viewed these mixed messages and wrote, "We need a framework which is consistent so that we do not say to one group of women, 'Biology is not destiny,' and to another, 'Alas, biology is destiny.' "[29]

Complex arguments and debates may persist, but individuals might cease to contradict themselves or cause wider confusion. Subscription to a comprehensive view of technological intervention in the womb will abet the philosophical integrity of feminisms by presenting thoughtful, consistent arguments instead of compartmentalized reactions. This integrity is important because it will foment the saliency of political agency and facilitate effective feminist response.

3. *The inevitable "advances" of medicine and technical invention demand comprehensive guidelines to enable immediate feminist responses.*

Human beings have always attempted to control fertility, infertility, pregnancy, and childbirth. In ancient Egypt, women placed dried crocodile dung next to the cervix to prevent conception,[30] and in sixteenth-century Greece, eating the uterus, testicle, and hoof paring of a mule was recommended.[31] Furthermore, unintended pregnancies were terminated through violent exercise, strong blows to the belly with rocks, sticks, or fists, and ingestion of an array of potions and potables. In fact, with the exception of injectable and embeddable hormonal prescriptives, all current contraceptives had already been invented by 1880. Simply, women have always tried to limit the number of children they produce.

Although different cultures and ages concocted different punishments for infertile women, all societies have deemed infertile women abnormal, leaving them desperate to become pregnant by almost any means necessary. In the Middle Ages, some women who failed to reproduce were burned as witches. "In centuries past, the woman who was childless was as useless and despised as a piece of land that would yield no crops. The same word was given to both—barren."[32] Women looked to magic and folklore for solutions to their infertility. They ate special foods, wore prescribed clothing, synchronized intercourse with the patterns of the moon and stars, and remained in bed for months at a time in hopes of conceiving successfully and giving birth. Women even hired or bribed other women to reproduce for them. The practice of surrogacy has existed for centuries and is even mentioned in the Bible story of Sarah and Hagar.[33] Women have been prepared to take drastic measures to reverse their infertility, just as other women were and are equally desperate to control their fertility.

Finally, human beings attempted to assert control during the prenatal and birth stages of pregnancy long before the creation of amniocentesis and epidurals. "Doctors" routinely prescribed a host of potables and practices in the name of fetal health and male offspring. Forceps, silver tongs used to pull the baby through the birth canal, are believed to have been created in the sixteenth century by the Chamberlen family:

> A mystique grew up around them: two of them attended at each difficult birth, arriving in a carriage and carrying between them a massive carved chest whose contents were revealed to

no one. Even the women they delivered were blindfolded. . . . This family Secret, kept for nearly a century, consisted of a kit of three instruments: a pair of obstetric forceps, a vectis or lever to be used in grasping the back of the head of the fetus, and a fillet or cord used to help in drawing the fetus, once disengaged from an abnormal position, out through the birth-canal.[34]

Interestingly, although human beings have been trying to mediate reproduction since the beginning of time, the only absolutely effective methods of pregnancy prevention remain abstinence, hysterectomy, and sterilization. Fifty-six percent of all pregnancies in the United States are unintended.[35] More than one in twelve married couples in the United States is infertile and maternal mortality, though rare, still occurs.[36]

While centuries of invention and experimentation have yet to reply completely to the mysteries of reproduction, we have come a long way. Most women no longer use crocodile dung or astrological intercourse to mediate their fertility and infertility. For example, there are now more than a dozen forms of female contraception, and several rival manufacturers of some devices and ingestives. Hysterectomy can now be performed vaginally rather than surgically. And several "new" technologies, from RU 486 (an oral abortificient) to self-administered anesthetics for use in childbirth, are being tested under a Federal Drug Administration (FDA)-approved protocol.

Moreover, like a snowball rolling down a hill and gathering snow along the way, the pace of progress in some areas is exponential.[37] After one discovery is made, a variety of commercial forms is manufactured and a host of related offspring is soon conceived. A good example of the rapid pace of development is the phenomenon of in vitro fertilization (IVF).

The first "test-tube" baby, Louise Brown, was born in 1978 in England. By December 1980, 278 women had participated in known experiments with IVF but only three gave birth, a mere 0.4 percent success rate. However, "teams" popped up everywhere—Canada, England, Australia, the United States—and what seemed to be a worldwide race began, a competition to see who could produce the most test-tube babies. Newspapers touted the births as sporting events with headlines such as, "Monash 8, Rest of the World 2."[38] By the mid-1980s, well over one hundred teams established clinics worldwide advertising infertility treatment, though only slightly more than two hundred test-tube babies had been produced.

In addition to a veritable plethora of IVF clinics sprouting everywhere, offshoots of in vitro fertilization were born. The first birth of a child conceived with a donated egg fertilized in vitro occurred in 1983 in Australia.[39] Shortly thereafter, complete "embryo adoption" (using both donated sperm and donated egg) became possible. On March 28, 1984, the first baby from a frozen and thawed IVF embryo was born.[40] "Embryo screening" for birth defects and sex also became possible, and most recently, "progress" has been made in genetic engineering, the adjusting of genetic makeup during the window period before embryo transfer and after fertilization. There are now more than three hundred clinics in the United States alone, which perform more than forty thousand IVFs and related procedures a year—a more than $350 million business.[41] Thus, only eighteen years after the first test-tube baby was born, the process exists worldwide and in a variety of forms.

Consequently, regardless of their effectiveness, forms of technological intervention in the womb have always existed and continue to exist. Some forms are not only growing but, as IVF experiments illustrate, they are multiplying at an increasing rate. If feminists intend to respond to these developments efficiently and consistently, a coherent set of standards against which specific new devices can be measured must be devised. The inevitable rate of progress makes it unfeasible to judge technologies reactively on a case-by-case basis.

Feminists need a set of principles and standards of which hospital boards, judges, the FDA, and politicians should be made aware before the invention, production, inspection, and legislation of new technologies. An inclusive paradigm needs to be established with respect to a feminist vision, instead of in response to a particular device. Janet Gallagher, an attorney with the American Civil Liberties Union (ACLU) Reproductive Freedom Project, argued for the need of an affirmative response to infertility treatments:

[F]eminists have all too often allowed ourselves to be driven into narrowly defensive, ultimately unsustainable public posi-

13

tions in which we seem to belittle both the pain of infertility and the satisfactions of motherhood. We have to learn better to avoid the media caricature of feminism that ignores our carefully wrought and balanced agendas. We need to project a vision that addresses the whole range of women's reproductive experiences, to publicly associate ourselves with affirmative proposals and demands supportive of a woman's choice . . .[42]

If feminists wish to control the development, administration, and availability of these technologies, it is vital that feminists create comprehensive positions on reproductive technology rather than defensive, piecemeal reactions.

4. The interdependent nature of technological intervention in the womb and the holistic reality of women's bodies and lives is best respected by a comprehensive approach.

Although rare, some contraceptive methods have rendered women sterile. For example, a notable potential side effect of IUD insertion, a once popular method of surgical contraception in the United States, is pelvic inflammatory disease, a common cause of infertility.[43] Women who seek infertility treatment (be it therapeutic donor insemination in any form, IVF in any form, or surrogacy) are more prone to use prenatal technologies. Moreover, these same women have a greater likelihood of Cesarean delivery. Helena Ragoné's study of both open and closed surrogacy programs in the United States demonstrates that most surrogacy programs require hospital birth. Further, interventive methods and medications are common (and often contracted) in surrogacy delivery. The use of prenatal technology has led to an increase in abortions motivated by the desire to select the sex of the child or to terminate an unhealthy fetus.[44] Simply, contraception may cause the need for infertility treatment, which tends to increase use of prenatal technologies. This, in turn, tends to increase the chance of either managed birth or abortion.

One example of the interconnected nature of these technologies was narrated in a *New York Times* series on infertility:

After Ms. Lee had endured at least 10 unsuccessful cycles of IVF and one ectopic pregnancy, doctors in 1992 fertilized her eggs with sperm from her husband in a petri dish and gingerly placed the embryos that resulted into Lee's uterus. Ms. Lee was born with a t-shaped uterus because of exposure to diethylstilbestrol, a hormone better know as DES that was widely prescribed to prevent miscarriages in the 1950's.[45]

Consequently, although the emotional and physical dilemmas are diverse, the same women (or their daughters)[46] may experience various technological interventions in their lifetimes because there is a causal relationship between many of these devices and prescriptions. Therefore, it is important to recognize these technologies as intimately related. For this reason, a single *medical* field has united all practices related to women's gynecological health and hygiene, as well as birth and its antecedents and sequels, under the umbrella of "gynecology and obstetrics." It is only logical that feminists treat these practices in a similarly realistic and comprehensive fashion.

I propose to recognize women as the logical epicenter of interconnected reproductive activity. In an article in the *Village Voice* on 16 July 1985, entitled "Putting Women Back into the Abortion Debate," Ellen Willis argued that the "debate over abortion—if not its reality—has become sexlessly scholastic." She lamented the fact that both left-wing and right-wing analysis was concerned with fetal viability, civil rights, economic realities, and so on, rather than the situation of specific women involved or the position of women in society more generally. She argued that discussion concerning abortion ought to focus upon women's biology and women's lives. Simply, she argued for a praxis feminism. Since the reality of women's bodies and lives is that we are multifaceted beings who may encounter a combination of technological interventions in the womb in our lifetimes, there is a need for a feminist response that is similarly capacious.[47]

In addition to the medical interconnectedness of technologies, feminists should consider the metaphysical interconnectedness of women's lives. Any discussion of reproductive technology necessarily implicates women's bodies and should consider the integrity of the entire unit. Dissecting a woman into particular organs and bodily functions is an unrealistic way of approaching women's lives and bodies. A woman's eggs exist within her ovaries, which are just another part of her entire body. Her body, in turn, should be viewed in the context of her livelihood, relationships, personality, and so on. Women should be viewed in the holistic fashion in which we actually exist. In *Woman and Nature: The Roaring Inside Her*, Susan Griffin advocates a form of understanding that she calls "synchronisities." This vision of women "involves the rejection and abolition of dualistic divisions and the creation of non-exploitative, non-hierarchical, reciprocal relationships between parts of our bodies and between women and nature."[48] Mary Daly also advocates perceiving the body in such a way as to recognize the entirety of the unit. In *Gyn/Ecology*, she calls this recognition of the natural interconnectedness of women's bodies and lives "gynaesthesia." This understanding of women's essence as being inherently bound with nature leads both Daly and Griffin to advance the cause of technophobia: artificial disruption of women's natural balance is deemed inherently antiwomen. While I believe that it is indeed necessary to view women's bodies and lives holistically, I do not think that this method of analysis necessarily dictates any specific ideology. It is possible to recognize the need for an expansive view of women and an inclusive view of reproductive technology, yet identify disparate feminist responses. Without necessarily embracing their ideology, I adopt the praxis method of analysis that values reality, viewing the woman as her body in the context of her life and society in general.

    5. All technological intervention in the womb is united in form.

    Although a tautology, it must be stated that all technological intervention in the womb is indeed a form of technology intervening in the womb; thus, the nature of technology itself deserves attention. Judy Wajcman identifies three related components of the term. First, technology is a form of practical knowledge. This "know-how" is sometimes unable to be verbalized, yet it is "visual, even tactile, and can also be systematized and taught."[49] Technology involves creative and innovative understanding in addition to academic scholarship (science): learning for the sake of doing, as opposed to knowledge for knowledge's sake. Second, technology refers to "what people do."[50] The actual application of "know-how" is a required element of technology: without the participation of the woman and the practitioner, forceps are merely bits of metal, and the knowledge of how to remove the fetus from the birth canal is useless. A set of human activities is clearly a required element of technology. Third, technology refers to the physical objects or "hardware" (such as the diaphragm, laparoscope, or hormonal drugs) that humans understand and manipulate. These objects can exist on a wide scale from natural (the use of seaweed as a cervical dilator) to artificial (a plastic diaphragm).

According to Wajcman's definition of technology, attempts to control fertility are related to attempts to control *in*fertility, monitor pregnancy, and manage birth, because all involve practical knowledge, application, and physical objects. All technological intervention in the womb represents the conscious attempt to alter the natural state of women's bodies and lives. Exactly who owns this power and the political implications of given technologies are sources of contention among feminists that will be explored in the chapters that follow. However, all feminists agree that technological intervention in the womb is what we might call "calculated"—an external object that is applied with requisite knowledge.

Moreover, these are technologies directed at women's bodies, technologies intended to alter reproduction and women's sexuality. Regardless of a particular response—whether we embrace or reject a particular entity—all technological interventions in the womb are materially similar. Thus, they should be judged by the same criteria.

Conclusion

In addition to these reasons, in the following chapters, it will become increasingly clear why I believe that in assessing the individual worth of these goods and services feminists should utilize a comprehensive view of technological intervention in the womb. Women's liberation will be facilitated by a practical and transcendent assessment of both technology and women.

What would this framework look like? Having considered the scope of technological intervention in the womb, the remainder of this book examines potential feminist frameworks, searching for a praxis feminist response to technological intervention in the womb.

Notes

1. "The Pill" is the term commonly used to describe oral hormonal ingestives. An entirely new method on the horizon is immunological contraception. See arti-

cles by both Judith Richter and Angeline Schrater in *Power and Decision: The Social Control of Reproduction*, Gita Sen and Rachel Snow, eds. (Boston: Harvard University Press, 1994). Also see Judith Richter, *Vaccination against Pregnancy: Miracle or Menace?* (London: Zed Books, 1996).

2. Although post-coital methods are not preventative measures, I include pregnancy termination under the rubric of contraception because all of these interventions involve the same desire: impeding unwanted pregnancy. I refer to "unwanted" pregnancy rather than "unplanned" pregnancy because I believe unwanted is a more inclusive term. A woman can plan a pregnancy but decide, for various reasons, not to continue it. Conversely, a pregnancy can be unplanned but wanted. Several court cases find a distinction between unwanted and unplanned: *Coleman v. Garrison*, 327 A.2d 757 (1974) (action by parents for damages alleging that doctor and hospital improperly performed on plaintiff wife a sterilization operation allowing her to become pregnant and deliver fifth child); *Rieck v. Medical Protective Co.*, 64 Wis. 2d 514, 219 N.W.2d 242 (1974) (parents brought action to recover costs of rearing child against clinic and ob/gyn who allegedly failed to determine pregnancy in time to permit termination); *White v. United States*, 510 F.Supp. 146 (1981) (alleging that Army physician negligently performed tubal ligation; the resulting child, his parents, and his siblings brought action); *Hartke v. McKelway*, 707 F.2d 1544, 228 U.S.App.D.C. 139 (1983) (wrongful conception case brought against surgeon who had performed laparoscopic cauterization in effort to prevent pregnancy of patient who later became pregnant and gave birth to healthy child). I thank Anne Oakley for convincing me of the need to clarify this distinction.

3. The Alan Guttmacher Institute, "Facts in Brief: Contraceptive Services" (1993).

4. The same transaction used to be called artificial or alternative insemination (with donor), but because of the similarity with the acronym AIDS, the term has been amended to TDI, or therapeutic donor insemination.

5. Felicia Lee, "The Fertility Market: Support and Solace," *The New York Times*, 9 January 1996, A1. This statistic included married couples who were unable to conceive naturally after one year of trying. In 1988, the Office of Technology and Assessment defined infertility as the inability to conceive naturally over a two-year period and declared infertility to affect an average of 2.4 million married couples. Clearly the definition of infertility significantly affects statistical data.

6. The Alan Guttmacher Institute, "Facts in Brief: Pregnancy and Birth in the United States" (1993).

7. Charity Scott, "Resisting the Temptation to Turn Medical Recommendations into Judicial Orders: A Reconsideration of Court-Ordered Surgery for Pregnant Women," *Georgia State Law Review* 10 (1994): 615–89, 662.

8. Charles Babington, "Abortion-Rights Group Broadens Focus," *The Washing-*

ton Post, 10 January 1993, A1. Also, during the health-care reform efforts in Washington, NARAL expanded its discussion to include "prenatal care," a concept that rhetorically fit pregnancy into debates about health care more generally. An editorial in *The Washington Post* praised NARAL for this expanded view: "Political maneuvers aside, the new stance happens to make a great deal of sense." See "Abortion Rights and Real Choice," *The Washington Post*, Opinion Editorial, 13 January 1994, A26.

9. For information on the significance of Catholic hospital mergers, see *Hospital Mergers: The Hidden Crisis for Family Planning*, published by Family Planning Advocates, 17 Elk Street, Albany, New York 12207.

10. Congregation for the Doctrine of Faith, "Instruction on Respect for Human Life in its Origin and on the Disunity of Procreation" (10 March 1981). Also, *Origins* 16 (19 March 1987): 698–711.

11. This point was reaffirmed in the 10 March 1987 Vatican statement titled, "Instruction on Respect for Human Life in its Origin and on the Destiny of Procreation: Replies to Certain Questions of the Day."

12. Pope Paul VI, "Encyclical Letter on the Regulation of Births," *Vatican Council II*, vol. 2 (25 July 1968): 397–408, 407. This encyclical established the two principles and was against contraception. The 1981 and 1987 statements dealt with IVF and TDI.

13. It is interesting to note that it is in part from this principle that rape is deemed sinful, not only because it is out of the bounds of matrimony, but also because it is a forced act as opposed to an act of willful unity.

14. Pope Paul VI, 407.

15. The Pope reaffirmed the importance of justice and chastity most recently in "Evangelium Vitae," released on 30 March 1995.

16. For example, see the tireless work of Catholics for a Free Choice (CFFC), led by Frances Kissling. CFFC literature stresses the fact that in Roman Catholicism there is a distinction between the teaching authority (*magisterium*) and the legislative function of the church, and the prohibition of abortion falls under the latter. Therefore, it is not governed by papal infallibility. See Jane Hurst, "The History of Abortion in the Catholic Church: The Untold Story," Abortion in Good Faith Series, published by Catholics for a Free Choice, Washington D.C., July 1989.

17. Gen. 1:28.

18. Rachel Biale, *Women and Jewish Law* (New York: Schocken Books, 1984), 198. I thank Jesse Furman for his insights and suggestions regarding women and Jewish law.

19. Biale, 136. Biale explains that *Halakhah* contends that regular sexual activity with the wife will prevent a man from committing adultery.

20. Biale, 121. *Onah* refers to the prescribed times for the husband to perform the conjugal duty. *Niddah* refers to the laws that proscribe sexual contact during and following menstruation.

21. Exod. 21:22–25.

22. Sandhedrin 72b.

23. Biale, 237.

24. "Orthodox Gains Trouble Women's Advocates," *Forward*, 26 July 1996, 2.

25. For a discussion of Islamic understanding of reproduction, see Carla Makhlouf Obermeyer, "Religious Doctrine, State Ideology and Reproductive Options in Islam," in *Power and Decision: The Social Control of Reproduction*, Gita Sen and Rachel Snow, eds. (Boston: Harvard University Press, 1994), 59–75. Obermeyer provides a bibliography for further reading on the subject.

26. Ruth Colker, *Abortion & Dialogue* (Bloomington: Indiana University Press, 1992), 100.

27. Robin Morgan, "Feminist Diplomacy," *Ms.* (May/June 1991): 1.

28. Rhonda Copelon, "From Privacy to Autonomy: The Conditions for Sexual and Reproductive Freedom," in *From Abortion to Reproductive Freedom: Transforming a Movement*, Marlene Gerber Fried, ed. (Boston: South End Press, 1990), 27–44.

29. Thelma McCormack, "When is Biology Destiny?" in *The Future of Human Reproduction*, Christine Overall, ed. (Toronto: The Women's Press, 1989), 84.

30. G. Zatuchni, "Current Problems in Obstetrics and Gynecology," as cited in Robert Crooks and Karla Baur, *Our Sexuality* (New York: Benjamin/Cummings Co., Inc., 1990), 356.

31. Crooks and Baur, 357.

32. Gena Corea, *The Mother Machine* (London: Women's Press, 1985), 15.

33. Sarah enlisted Hagar, a slave-girl, to produce a child (Ishmael) for Abraham (Gen. 16:1–15). I will discuss the classist overtones of surrogacy in chapter 5.

34. Adrienne Rich, *Of Woman Born* (New York: W. W. Norton, 1976), 143.

35. The Alan Guttmacher Institute, "Facts in Brief: Contraceptive Services" (1993). A 1996 paper by Sylvia Law presented at the Bellagio Conference, "Access to Reproductive Drugs and Devices," examines several potential reasons for the relatively few contraceptive methods available in the United States. On file with the author.

36. The maternal mortality rate (number of deaths to women from complications of pregnancy and childbirth per hundred thousand live births) dropped from 9.2 in 1980 to 7.9 in 1989. The maternal mortality rate for black women (18.4) is double that of Hispanic women (9.2) and more than triple that of white women (5.6). The Alan Guttmacher Institute, "Facts in Brief: Pregnancy and Birth in the United States" (1993).

37. It was suggested to me that the snowball analogy might be inappropriate because sometimes snowballs melt when they get to a warm part on the hill. However, several technologies have indeed "melted" after enjoying great spurts of popularity such as the Dalkon Shield, Benedictin, and so on.

38. This headline appeared in *The Age* (25 June 1981), and was cited by Corea at

118. Monash University in Australia had an extremely prolific team headed by Dr. Carl Wood.

39. Corea, 125.

40. Corea, 118. Not surprisingly, this woman had a Cesarean section delivery. See the argument that follows describing the synergistic relationship of reproductive technologies.

41. Trip Gabriel, "The Fertility Market: High-Tech Pregnancies Test Hope's Limit," *The New York Times*, 7 January 1996, A1.

42. Janet Gallagher, "Eggs, Embryos and Foetuses: Anxiety and the Law," in *Reproductive Technologies: Gender, Motherhood, and Medicine*, Michelle Stanworth, ed. (Cambridge: Polity Press, 1987), 139–50, 149.

43. For an explanation of the relationship between IUDs and pelvic inflammatory disease (PID), a common cause of infertility, see Corea, 161–62. Because of the several public lawsuits surrounding the Dalkon Shield, an IUD that was found to have caused an alarming number of cases of PID, it is no longer widely used in the United States, though it is still a popular method of pregnancy prevention worldwide.

44. Of women having abortions, 1 percent had been advised that the fetus had a defect and an additional 12 percent feared that the fetus may have been harmed by medications or other conditions. The Alan Guttmacher Institute, "Facts in Brief: Abortion in the United States" (1995).

45. Elizabeth Rosenthal, "The Fertility Market: From Lives Begun in a Lab," *The New York Times*, 10 January 1996, A1. The author's reference to "gingerly" placing the embryos into the surrogate is a good example of the kind of romantic and inaccurate normative language typically used with respect to infertility treatments, which is addressed in chapter 4: can technological interventions ever be "gingerly" placed in a woman's womb?

46. DES, a synthetic estrogen that was first created in a British lab by Sir Charles Dodds in 1938, was administered orally and produced cheaply for several decades in the middle of this century. Although the drug was meant to prevent miscarriage, studies proved it ineffective and, more important, offspring were noted to have had problems varying from cancer to infertility as a result of maternal ingestion. See section one, in *The Custom-Made Child?*, Helen Holmes, Betty Hoskins, Michael Gross, eds. (Clifton, N.J.: Humana Press, 1981). Also see Harriet Simand, "1938–1988: Fifty Years of DES—Fifty Years Too Many," in *The Future of Human Reproduction*, Christine Overall, ed. (Toronto: The Women's Press, 1989), 95–104.

47. Also see Mary Mahowald, "As if There Were Fetuses Without Women: A Remedial Essay," in *Reproduction, Ethics and the Law: Feminist Perspectives*, Joan Callahan, ed. (Bloomington: Indiana University Press, 1995), 199–218. She argues for a woman-centered approach to fetal tissue transplantation.

48. Maggie Humm, *The Dictionary of Feminist Theory* (London: Harvester Wheatsheaf, 1989), 98.

49. Judy Wajcman, *Feminism Confronts Technology* (Cambridge: Polity Press, 1991), 14.

50. Wajcman, 14. Therefore, she distinguishes between this creative understanding and innovative application that characterizes technology, and the purely intellectual understanding that is science. Rather than viewing technology and science as hierarchical, she claims that this relationship is interactive and symmetrical.

2

TECHNOPHILIA

*I*s technological intervention in the womb the friend or foe of women? This chapter examines the theories of two feminists—Shulamith Firestone and Donna Haraway—as constructed examples of views that embrace reproductive technology as the ally of women in our struggle for gender justice. Because they are enthusiastic about the supposedly emancipatory nature of technology, I call these two theorists "technophiles."[1]

Not all people who endorse legal and available technological intervention in the womb are "technophiles." Chapter 5 explores the privacy approach to technology, a liberal tradition that values access to technology as a consequence of its commitments to individual rights.

Technophilia involves embracing technological innovation itself, reverence for the ability to control and explain nature. Accordingly, all things mechanical are due greater respect than all things natural because nature is imperfect, inefficient, and untamed.

Very few technophiles are feminists. For an extreme example, Adolf Hitler advocated the application of reproductive technology toward the creation of a master race. Although this chapter refers to "technophiles," it examines the theoretical reasons for *feminist* technophilia; veneration for technology because of the belief that it will free women from the burden of reproduction, the primary source of our oppression.

Finally, not all (feminist) technophiles audit reproductive technology. There are several recent publications regarding women and domestic technology as well as women and military technology.[2] However, I ask what vision of women, sexual oppression, and technology could inspire people to embrace technological intervention in the womb in the name of feminism?

In 1949 Simone de Beauvoir published *The Second Sex* in which she explained the origins and tyranny of women's "otherness." She claimed that women are socialized as beings whose existence directly contrasts that of men.[3] As the "other" sex, women are deemed passive and uncreative, excluded from public life. Although de Beauvoir described the inert state of the egg and the passive acceptance on the part of the womb of the traveling, ambitious sperm, she did not attribute women's second-class status solely to biology, but also to the institutions and social conditions, such as women's unpaid, repetitive, and monotonous domestic labors, which enforce sex-based oppression. In her words, "One is not born, one becomes a woman."[4] Despite this recognition of systematic patriarchy, she also recognized the female body itself as a source of sociopolitical frustration, advocating legal abortion and contraception as a means of controlling difference and achieving liberation. Although de Beauvoir did not name the body as the sole source of women's subjection, it was her evident cynicism toward the body that inspired Shulamith Firestone's advocacy of ectogenesis—reproduction that occurs completely outside any biological body, the replication of human life void of human host and participation—to which I now turn.

In 1970, Shulamith Firestone published *The Dialectic of Sex* in which she outlined her approach to women's liberation. Building from the suspicion of the female body presented by de Beauvoir (she even dedicates her book to de Beauvoir), Firestone claimed that it is "women's reproductive biology that accounts for her original and continued oppression":[5]

> Throughout history, in all stages and types of culture, women have been oppressed due to their biological functions.[6]

In addition to viewing women's reproductive capacity as a source of hardship in itself, Firestone noted that this biological reality necessarily, both as a matter of logic and as a fact of history, leads to the creation of "family structures which are inherently unequal power distributions."[7] Thus, biological sex determines one's position in the family and society as either privileged and male or oppressed and female. It is important to place Firestone within the tradition of radical feminism at large.

Radical Feminism

The word "radical" used in association with any political group is usually associated with views, practices, and policies of extreme change. It is often used by journalists or politicians to discredit and automatically dismiss individuals and organizations as "fringe" leftists (or rightists, for that matter). I do not use the term "radical" disparagingly. Indeed, many of the pioneers of women's rights—from the Pankhursts to Margaret Sanger—were radical activists or extremists. However, in feminist theory, "radical" has another definition that focuses on feminist substance rather than form: "of, relating to, or proceeding from the root or origin."[8] Radical feminism refers to a body of thought with particular views about the origin of women's oppression: the male-supremacist sex-class system.[9] Simply, there is a difference between radical feminist method and radical feminist thought, and it is the latter that is the focus of this chapter (and the next chapter as well).

Most of those whom I call radical feminists believe that sex, the division of society into the categories of men and women, is the most significant factor of women's oppression and liberation. They believe in the existence of a vital sex-class system at the expense of other significant social divisions such as class, race, age, and so on. When asked, "What are women?" radical feminists presume to be able to respond with confidence, "Women are X": they have a "fixed essence."[10] Three forms of radical feminism deserve further attention.

Feminists such as Susan Griffin are commonly described as biologically determined essentialists because they determine women's nature to be the result of physiological structure. Women are women because our bodies are female: we are physically supine, soft, receptive, and, most notably, we have the capacity to reproduce. Griffin analogizes women to nature and Mother Earth:

> We are the bird's eggs. Bird's eggs. Flowers, butterflies, rabbits, cows, sheep; we are caterpillars; we are leaves of ivy and sprigs of wallflower.

We are women. We rise from the wave. We are gazelle and doe, elephant and whale, lilies and roses and peach, we are air, we are flame, we are oyster and pearl, we are girls. We are woman and nature. And he says he cannot hear us speak.[11]

Like Griffin, Jane Alpert, in her famous 1973 letter from underground that appeared in *Ms.* magazine, ascribed women's attitudes and abilities to our material selves with particular attention to the female capacity to have children. She argued that female biology gives rise to psychological powers that shape our unique perspective as women.[12] Firestone's attention to sexual reproduction places her in the company of other biological essentialists like Griffin and Alpert. However, biological essentialists not only refer to reproductive organs, but also to neurology, neurophysiology, and endocrinology as physical sources of gendered essence. Thus, these feminists believe that "biology constitutes an unalterable bedrock of identity."[13]

Naturalist essentialists may defer to biology, but they also consider theological or ontological reasons for gender distinctions. Mary Daly's references to women's innate spirituality are attributed to her recognition of genital morphology, God-given traits, or a combination of the two. However, this spiritual dimension of life is not based on Christianity, Judaism, or Islam, but on a Goddess-based religion. Daly calls this the "female principle," a notion that has been reinforced by many radical feminists since its conception. In the words of Vandana Shiva and Maria Mies: "Spirituality is largely identical to women's sensuality, their sexual energy, their most precious life force which links them to each other, to other life forms, and the elements. It is the energy that enables women to love and celebrate life."[14] While this spirituality is intimately connected with women's biology, the naturalist contends that the link between women's physical being and essence is more complicated than the biologist's contention that physical reality simply equals essence. The naturalist claims that there is an additional link in the chain of explanation such that biology is related to female spirituality, which in turn fosters essence.

Finally, some feminists, such as de Beauvoir, argue that women's otherness is socially constructed. De Beauvoir's statement that "one is not born, one becomes a woman" credits institutions such as the family, work, education, art, and literature with molding a woman's own identity as well as her social position as "feminine." All social constructionists view patriarchy[15] as a powerful force shaping women's otherness, yet radical social constructionists view patriarchy as omnipresent and inevitable.[16] For example, Nancy Chodorow attributes masculine and feminine personality roles to the fact that women are largely responsible for early childcare.[17] Kate Millett recognizes the significance of psychosocial conditioning at the hands of patriarchal structures, focusing on education, the family, and class as agents of oppression.[18] Juliet Mitchell censures economic structures and bourgeois ideology for having created gender inequality.[19] Consequently, although focusing on different examples and disparate specific sources, radical constructionists claim that it is women's experience, indeed our very existence, in the context of patriarchy that constructs difference.

Of course, there are social constructionists who are not radical feminists, such as Zillah Eisenstein and Rosalind Petchesky, who will be discussed in later chapters. These liberal social constructionists see legal reform as a means of altering presently rigid gender distinctions and experiences. Simply, liberal social constructionists see social reform as possible, while radical social constructionists view gender differences as universal, inevitable, and permanent. This chapter confronts only radical feminist visions.

Some feminists contend that radical feminisms are mutually exclusive and in conflict with each other. For example, Adrienne Rich suggests that social constructionism and biological essentialism are opposing visions. She contends that because the social forces that construct an oppressive conception of gender are extremely pervasive, short of a complete upheaval and social revolution (which many do advocate), lesbian separatism is a means of avoiding gender oppression. Rich argues that the creation of a lesbian continuum is a viable plan of escape from the feminine/masculine dichotomy. She writes, "Lesbian existence comprises both the breaking of a taboo and the rejection of a compulsory way of life. . . . We may first begin to perceive it as a form of nay-saying to patriarchy, a form of resistance."[20] The contention that a biological female can avoid essentialism by avoiding social construction does suggest that the social constructionist is at odds with the biologist and naturalist explanations of essentialism. (Imagine a biological female alone in the Sahara from the moment of birth. Does she display feminine essence? Is she a woman?) Many separatist communes exhibit eco/peace/feminine political natures. However, complete separatism, the complete rejection of society, is not a readily viable option for most women.[21]

I contend that biological, natural, and constructionist radical feminisms are not necessarily mutually exclusive visions, as none fundamentally denies the other. As noted earlier, the biological and naturalist stances not only can coexist, but potentially reinforce each other. Further, Rosalind Coward argues that naturalism and social construction are actually forms of biologism, since who is "made" man and who is "made" woman are based upon assumptions about and determinations of sex, as males are typically socialized as men and females as women:

> How is it that a society unilaterally affects anatomical women in one way and anatomical men in another way? And what is it about that anatomical state which guarantees that anatomical men and women will consistently take up these roles, as social men and women?[22]

Moreover, some theorists are difficult to categorize as one type or another. For example, some claim that Luce Irigaray argues that women have a biologically coded femininity and that this essence is suppressed by present dominant forms of speech and writing. She (also) argues that language should allow women not only to express ourselves as women, but also to discover our sexuality. Consequently, language is both a function of innate difference and a means to create difference: much debate ensues regarding whether Luce Irigaray is a constructionist or a biological essentialist.[23]

Contemplate categorization of Mary Daly. She is often cited as the quintessential natural essentialist, yet her condemnation of language as an instrument of patriarchy (a social construction) compelled her to create a feminist dictionary, *Webster's First New Intergalactic Wickedry of the English Language* (1987), and a new language based on gynaesthesia.

Finally, consider Carol Gilligan. Her psychological study of women's development—specifically, the relation between judgment and action in a situation of moral conflict and choice—documented the distinct sound of women's voice. Her research suggested that women rely on an ethic of care in decision making, while men are more concerned with justice. However, in the introduction to *In a Different Voice*, Gilligan explains that she makes "no claims . . . about the origins of the differences described."[24] Consequently, it is unclear what kind of feminist Gilligan is, though she explicitly ascribes to an understanding of gender difference.

From the perspective of a discussion of radical feminism, it does not matter whether a particular radical feminist is an essentialist or a radical constructionist or whether particular radical feminisms are mutually exclusive. My explication of three types of radical feminism was an effort to briefly highlight the richness of (radical) feminism and the difficulty (indeed, absurdity?) of being overly focused upon classification rather than praxis. For whatever reason and in whatever form, Irigaray, Daly, and other radical feminists subscribe to a strong notion of difference between women and men—which is why radical feminists are often described as "difference" feminists. They believe that gender is a sex-class system that is inevitable, permanent, and universal—women of all times and places constitute a caste. Sisterhood is ubiquitous.

> [Radical feminism] entails the belief that those characteristics defined as women's essence are shared in common by all women at all times: it implies a limit on the variations and possibilities of change—it is not possible for a subject to act in a manner contrary to her nature. . . . [Radical feminism] thus refers to the existence of fixed characteristics, given attributes and ahistorical functions.[25]

Shulamith Firestone

Like her radical sisters, Firestone understood difference as the main source of women's oppression. However, she then deemed women's bodies anathema.

Applying Marxist analysis to the sexual oppression of women, Firestone advocated eradicating sex-based oppression by toppling sexual distinction itself.[26] Marx and Engels argued that liberation of the proletariat required eliminating unequal ownership of the means of production, the source of class division. It was not only the mere possession of private property that inspired societal stratification, but the use of these commodities and the consequent identification of people in relation to these goods.

> Private property has made us so stupid and one-sided that an object is only ours when we have it—when it exists for us as capital, or when it is directly possessed, eaten, drunk, worn, inhabited, etc.—in short, when it is *used* by us. . . . In place of all these physical and mental senses therefore come the sheer estrangement of all these senses—the sense of having. . . . The transcendence of human property is therefore the complete emancipation of all human senses and attributes.[27]

Similarly, according to Firestone, female and male sexual genitalia could still exist, but the reproductive meaning of these organs would be eliminated, since it is human reproductive capacity that creates gender identification and thus division. Thanks to technology, reproduction would become a public commodity.

> [A]nd just as the end goal of the socialist revolution was not only the elimination of the economic class privilege but of the economic class distinction itself, so the end goal of the feminist revolution must be . . . not just the elimination of male privilege but of the sex distinction itself: genital differences between human beings would no longer matter culturally. . . . The reproduction of the species by one sex for the benefit of both would be replaced by (at least the option of) artificial reproduction.[28]

Thus, technology should be worshipped as a revolutionary force that delivers women from the tyranny of biological sex. Through ectogenesis, sexual reproduction is eliminated. Once the reproductive meaning of sexual difference is erased, equality (of result) can be established. Women will not become men; rather, these distinctions will be completely destroyed, and people will be recognized only as human beings. Sex as an activity might still be practiced, but it will be void of any reproductive meaning.[29] Consequently, sexual equality is established at the expense of biological reproduction itself.

Inspired by Firestone's analysis of women's oppression and her ectogenic prescription for liberation, Marge Piercy wrote *Woman on the Edge of Time* in 1979.[30] In this novel, Connie is an emotionally and physically abused woman who is locked away in a mental institution. Unable to escape physically, her only refuge is drifting into the future mentally. She and Luciente are telepaths able to "catch" each other in their respective times. Luciente's future is Firestone's utopia, a society of complete social and ecological harmony. Private ownership is nonexistent, coupling takes place among individuals rather than sexual categories (men-women or women-women or men-men), and human and non-human animals enjoy understanding through sign language. Crucial to the establishment of such a utopia was the destruction of sexual reproduction, as Luciente explains to Connie:

> It was part of women's long revolution. When we were breaking all the old hierarchies. Finally there was that one thing we had to give up too, the only power we ever had, in return for no more power for anyone. The original production: the power to give birth. Cause as long as we were biologically enchained, we'd never be equal. And males never would be humanized to be loving and tender. So we all became mothers. Every child has three. To break the nuclear bonding.[31]

Although Luciente's technologically driven future represents something desirable, a place where justice is not a political ideal but a reality, Piercy acknowledges the potential of technology to create disharmony and inequality, if employed unjustly. In the present day, Connie's doctors are determined to implant electronic devices in the brains of patients, regardless of whether they require such drastic intervention. The doctors are obsessed with exercising control and power over the patients. Ironically, Connie's one problem is that she lacks self-determination, and the doctors' use of medication and intervention serves only to accentuate that imperfection. Thus, Piercy warns that technology does not necessarily emancipate women, but that it is potentially liberating or detrimental, depending upon the conditions of its use and allocation.

Piercy not only recognizes the possible negative implications of technology in the present day, but she also laments its lethal potential to shape the future negatively, as Connie mistakenly "catches" a glimpse of New York City on one visit forward. This place represents Firestone's dystopia. The categories of male-female and rich-poor are no longer merely subconsciously reinforced by cultural tradition and social expectation; they are mandated and promulgated outwardly by law. In the future, present evils such as housing inequities and prostitution are exaggerated to the extent that the poor never see the sky and contracts for women sex-slaves restrict them to single rooms for two years or more. Via her futuristic depiction of New York City, Piercy acknowledges that a struggle between good and evil surrounds technology in all times. Technology is potentially as integral to a dystopia as it is to Firestone's utopia. As Luciente explained, "It's that race between technology, in the service of those who control, and insurgency—those who want to change the society in our direction."[32] Consequently, although Piercy's description of Firestone's utopia is enviable, as Connie remains in the clutches of the mental institution at the close of the book, one is left skeptical that the struggle that surrounds science will ever be happily or at least easily solved. Piercy's message is one of cynicism: Firestone's hopes and dreams provide the foundation for an interesting science fiction, but an unlikely reality.

Donna Haraway

A biologist by training, Donna Haraway, too, has contemplated the creation of a post-gender world in her acclaimed narrative "Manifesto for Cyborgs: Science, Technology and Socialist Feminism."[33] While Firestone's utopia depends upon in vitro genesis, Haraway argues that humans are fast becoming, and inevitably will be, "a cybernetic organism . . . a hybrid of machine and organism, a creature of social reality as well as a creature of fiction."[34] Haraway styles herself as less of a dreamer than Firestone. Instead, she claims to predict the future. She argues that human evolution includes the incorporation of technology. We presently ingest food additives and vitamins regularly, and the sick receive artificial limbs and organs, but Haraway argues that eventually all human beings, the healthy as well as unhealthy, will be mechanical hybrids.

So called "cyborgs" are self-replicating beings for whom reproduction is an asexual undertaking:

> Unlike the hopes of Frankenstein's monster, the cyborg does
> not expect his father to save it through the restoration of the
> Garden; that is, through the fabrication of a heterosexual mate.
> . . . The cyborg does not dream of community on the model of
> the organic family.[35]

Cyborgs do not possess in any way the problematic dualisms present
in Western society of boy-girl, public-private, natural-artificial, and
so on. Moreover, cyborgs do not possess the ultimate dualistic identity, masculine-feminine. The cyborg "entails the sticking together
of incongruous and seemingly antagonistic elements in order to create new and different patterns."[36] Because of technological innovation, people are no longer human beings, but rather self-sufficient
information systems, texts, and ergonomically controlled laboring,
desiring, and reproducing objects. Embracing technology, Haraway
welcomes the ultimate self-determining agent:

> [Cyborgs have] no seductions to organic wholeness through a
> final appropriation of all the powers of the parts into original
> higher unity . . . it is the awful apocalyptic *telos* of the West's
> escalating dominations of abstract individualism . . . the myth
> of the original unity, fullness, bliss and terror represented by
> the phallic mother from whom all humans must separate.[37]

Technology will deliver women into a state of being where the category "women" is of only historical relevance. In the mechanical
realm, people are *individuals*, capable of exercising their privileges
as citizens and acting on independent desires free from the construct of gender. Rather than constructing a liberatory ethos around
the politics of shared identity, Haraway, like Firestone, creates coali-
tions centered around actual affinity, a literal caste of people or,
more accurately, a literal caste of cyborgs.[38] In compliance with the
ideology of both Marx and Firestone, Haraway resolves sexual difference by eliminating the source of the problem itself.

However, in contrast to Firestone, Haraway describes a cyborg
who is "neither good nor bad, but simply, if confusingly, there."[39]
In describing what she argues is an inevitability, she acknowledges

the potential constraints of technology as a utopic replacement for sexual reproduction: "Who controls the interpretation of bodily boundaries in medical hermeneutics is a major feminist issue."[40] Thus, she concedes the possibility of androcentrism in the cybernetic universe. The sex-free state may not be free of hierarchy. Recognizing that despotism may penetrate her technological milieu, she argues that women must "refuse anti-science metaphysics" and instead "embrace the task of reconstruction."[41] In other words, the cyborg future is inevitable; therefore, women should embrace it and put ourselves in positions whereby we can influence and control its meaning.[42] Consequently, Haraway argues for "pleasure in the confusion of boundaries *and* responsibility in their confusion,"[43] both of which can only occur because of technological progress.

Critique of Technomania

Critics such as Mary Anne Doane are skeptical of the possibility of constructing a gender-neutral cybernetic state. Doane argues that Haraway "dehistoricizes [technological development]—a high-tech society somehow marks a complete break with the society and the dualisms that precede it."[44] Yet, is it possible for a mechanical-organic hybrid seemingly created by humans (as opposed to miraculously appearing from the heavens) to be void of all human subjectivity? Can any object created in an impure climate truly be pure? Doane argues that any discussion of loss, absence, and difference is completely missing from the cybernetic state. Consequently, like Firestone, Haraway does not adequately address the likelihood of enduring inequality, perhaps reinforced inequality, in her postgender world.

Besides the prospect of androcentric creation and administration of cybernetics and ectogenesis, there are many other drawbacks to these approaches. Practically speaking, more than twenty-five years after Firestone's ideas were first published, although scientists claim to be edging nearer a time when conception, fertilization, and full development of the fetus will exist entirely in vitro, non-human reproduction is not yet possible. Although conception and fertilization can occur in vitro, with the greatest medical assistance the fetus can survive outside the womb only from approximately twenty-two weeks.[45] In fact, the closest manifestation of an artificial womb is the "extrauterine fetal incubator" created by researchers in Tokyo. "They have taken goat fetuses, threaded catheters through the large vessels in the umbilical cord and supplied the fetuses with oxygenated blood while suspending them in incubators that contain artificial amniotic fluid heated to body temperature."[46] Thus, artificial human gestation has yet to be invented, let alone an artificial womb that could be widely distributed and marketed such that natural gestation became obsolete. Also, scientists have yet to create eggs artificially. Thus, as the sole producers of eggs and possessors of wombs, women are still a vital element of reproduction. Furthermore, even if artificial eggs and wombs were created (or discovered), men are still needed for production of sperm. Although "sperm banks" exist, men are still indispensable (as they make "deposits") and as long as men as a sex category have a reproductive function, sexual difference persists. In short, while either males or females are still required for reproduction, sexual meaning continues. Because technology must be completely comprehensive to eradicate the social meaning of sexual difference, and because the possibility of completely artificial creation or independent replication is still very much in the distant scientific future, Firestone and Haraway provide only marginally practical prescriptions for liberation.

Furthermore, many argue that the very pursuit of ectogenesis and cybernetics only further oppresses women, since our complicity is required for experimentation, and present research methods can involve pain and harmful side effects.[47] An article in *Glamour* magazine (May 1994) described one woman's uncomfortable experience with egg donation. Gwen Martin wrote, "I imagined injecting myself with hormones over the next weeks. And suddenly I saw those needles as a perfect metaphor for the invasion to which I was subjecting myself. . . . Despite my misgivings, and the persistent feeling that I was being taken advantage of, I continued in the program." Martin eventually left the donor program. This short-term degradation might be endurable if the ends were to justify the means. However, the basic assumption that sexual (reproductive) dualism is the sole (or even significant) source of women's oppression is open to challenge.

Women's inequality can be attributed to a multiplicity of factors (such as the family, educational inequity, religion, and so on), as Firestone's mentor, de Beauvoir, recognized in her chronicle of oppressive social agents; and Haraway concedes that women should enter the sciences in order to help shape the cyborg future. While the many other agents of oppression may in fact be influenced or even grounded upon biological difference, it is unclear how eradication of sexual reproduction will manage to erase these other despotic forces. Would ectogenesis truly mean that all children would be treated in the same manner in classrooms? Would ectogenesis spontaneously end sexual harassment and unequal pay scales in the workplace? Firestone's prescription for liberation, which focuses upon obliterating biological difference (and specifically the reproductive aspects of biology), presents an overly simplistic approach to such pervasive inequality.

Firestone, in particular, is criticized by other radical feminists for not recognizing the positive aspects of women's biological capacity. As I will suggest in chapter 3, many feminists revere the experience of childbirth as liberating.[48] Feminists such as Susan Griffin and Mary Daly celebrate the womb as a source of power and sisterhood. Moreover, Firestone's loathing of the female body and Haraway's embrace of a post-sexual difference world of cyborgs are liberation through disassociation with the body, which Elizabeth Spelman argues aligns feminists with centuries of male somatophobia, fear of and disdain for the body:

> The responsibility for being embodied creatures has been assigned to women: we have been associated, indeed virtually identified, with the body: men (or some men) have been associated and virtually identified with the mind. Women have been portrayed as possessing bodies in ways that men do not. It is as if women essentially, men only accidentally, have bodies. . . . Firestone's prescription does not challenge the negative attitude towards the body; it only hopes to end the association between the body, so negatively characterized, and women.[49]

Conclusion

If different biology is the fundamental cause of social inequities (and I have presented a few of the feminist arguments that doubt this contention), and yet sexual reproduction is inescapable, can liberation ever be attained? Defining oppression as sexual difference and liberation as equality of result (meaning, we will only be equal when we are exactly the same) dictates the impossibility of our deliverance.

Although these theories may not be practical, it is provocative and helpful to contemplate the ectogenic utopia designed by Firestone and explained by Piercy, and the hopeful predictions of Haraway. Extracted elements of Firestone and Haraway are extremely relevant: the importance of reproductive capacity, the inevitability of technological invention and intervention, and so on. Any praxis-oriented feminism should be cognizant of these insightful suppositions.

If we accept that sexual difference is both meaningful and inescapable, must this difference be denounced? Rather, a viable prescription for liberation might find power in difference. The following chapter will describe radical feminists who have positive understandings of difference.

Notes

1. Carol A. Stabile introduced the terms "technomania" and "technophobia" in her book *Feminism and the Technological Fix* (Manchester, England: Manchester University Press, 1994). I found this book highly compelling. However, I think technomania has a negative connotation, implying irrationality. I prefer the term "technophilia" to describe pro-technology sentiment. Becky Holmes and Ivan Zimmerman were helpful with this decision.

2. Judy Wajcman includes a comprehensive bibliography that should be consulted for further reading in this area.

3. For further discussion of the problems associated with the creation of binary opposites—identities constructed in dichotomies—see the work of Jacques Derrida listed in the bibliography.

4. Simone de Beauvoir, *The Second Sex* (Harmondsworth: Penguin, 1953), 57.

5. Shulamith Firestone, *The Dialectic of Sex* (London: The Women's Press, 1970), 74–75.

6. Firestone, 74–75.

7. Firestone, 17.

8. Noah Webster, *Webster's Seventh New Collegiate Dictionary* (Springfield, Mass.: G & C Merriam Company, 1967), 705.

9. It is true that some radical feminists are also radical radical feminists, or what we might call "extreme" because they demand dramatic upheaval. Moreover, the liberal and materialist feminists explored in subsequent chapters may also call for sweeping revolution.

10. Elizabeth Grosz, "Sexual Difference and the Problem of Essentialism," in *The Essential Difference*, Naomi Schor and Elizabeth Weed, eds. (Bloomington: Indiana University Press, 1994), 82–97, 84.

11. Susan Griffin, *Woman and Nature: The Roaring Inside Her* (New York: Perennial Library, 1978), 1.

12. Jane Alpert, "Mother Right: A New Feminist Theory," part I and II, *Ms.* (August 1973): 52–55, 88–94. Alpert was wanted by federal investigators for her alleged connection to several politically motivated bombings in New York. In the August 1973 *Ms.*, the introduction by Gloria Steinem and part I further explain her underground existence.

13. Grosz, 85.

14. Maria Mies and Vandana Shiva, *Ecofeminism* (London: Zed Books, 1993), 17.

15. Patriarchy refers to structural male domination. It is characterized by dualisms and divisions, hierarchies that favor male authority and privilege. Mary Daly argues that patriarchy is the prevailing religion of civilization and it is ahistorical and universal. Mary Daly, *Beyond God the Father: Toward a Philosophy of Women's Liberation* (Boston: Beacon, 1973). *Gyn/Ecology: The Metaethics of Radical Feminism* (Boston: Beacon, 1978). *Pure Lust: Elemental Feminist Philosophy* (Boston: Beacon, 1984).

16. See A. Brah, "Questions of Difference and International Feminism," in *Out of the Margins*, J. Aaron and S. Walby, eds. (London: Falmer, 1991).

17. Nancy Chodorow, *The Reproduction of Mothering* (Berkeley: University of California Press, 1978).

18. Kate Millett, *Sexual Politics* (New York: Doubleday, 1970).

19. Juliet Mitchell, "Women and Equality," in *Feminism and Equality*, Anne Phillips, ed. (New York: New York University Press, 1987), 24–43.

20. Adrienne Rich, "Compulsory Heterosexuality and Lesbian Existence," *Signs* 5 (1983): 631–60. Also see the work of Ti-Grace Atkinson who argued that "feminism is the theory, lesbianism is the practice" in *Amazon Odyssey* (New York: Links, 1974).

21. Diana Fuss argues that some radical constructionists believe that patriarchy is so pervasive that the idea of essence itself is a social construction. According to Fuss, constructionists "reject the idea that any essential or natural givens precede the processes of social determination." (See Locke's description of real and nominal essences for strict constructionist visions.) Thus, it would seem that constructionists might reject the contentions of biological and natural essentialists. However, both Fuss and Rosalind Coward contend that "social constructionists do not definitively escape the pull of essentialism . . . indeed essentialism subtends the

very idea of constructionism." For further discussion, see Diana Fuss, *Essentially Speaking: Feminism, Nature and Difference* (New York: Routledge, 1989), and Rosalind Coward, *Patriarchal Precedents: Sexuality and Social Relations* (London: Routledge, 1983).

22. Coward, 267.

23. See Naomi Schor, "This Essentialism Which Is Not One: Coming to Grips with Irigaray," in *The Essential Difference*, Naomi Schor and Elizabeth Weed, eds. (Bloomington: Indiana University Press, 1994), 40–62.

24. Carol Gilligan, *In a Different Voice* (Cambridge: Harvard University Press, 1982), 2.

25. Grosz, 84.

26. Firestone herself is careful to note that it is Marx and Engels' methodology only that she co-opts, since women were never a feminist-identified subject matter in Marxism. She writes, "For feminist revolution we shall need an analysis of the dynamics of sex war as comprehensive as the Marx-Engels analysis of class antagonism was for the economic revolution. . . . In creating such an analysis we can learn a lot from Marx and Engels: not their literal opinions about women—about the condition of women as an oppressed class they know next to nothing, recognizing it only where it overlaps with economics—but rather their analytic *method.*" Firestone, 12.

27. Karl Marx, "Economic and Philosophic Manuscripts of 1844: Private Property and Communism," in *The Marx-Engels Reader*, Robert C. Tucker, ed. (London: W.W. Norton, 1978), 87. Marx's suspicion of capitalism and private ownership first appeared in his essay, "On the Jewish Question," written in 1843, in which he called for the emancipation of society from Judaism—a word that he used interchangeably with "huckstering" and later with "capitalism."

28. Firestone, 19.

29. Although beyond the scope of this project, it is interesting to note the implications of this approach in the context of discrimination based upon sexual orientation. In Firestone's utopia, the law and society more generally might finally accept the notion of love and sexual relations among individuals rather than binary opposites.

30. One of the earliest feminist scientific utopias is Rokeya Sukhawat Hossain's *Sultana's Dream*. In an introduction to excerpts from this book, Frances Bonner wrote, "It does not matter that the technology described is impossible; it is based on such scientific principles as were known to a (self-)educated Bengali woman at the turn of the century. . . . The story provides a remarkably early instance of the identification of 'bad' male science with weaponry and 'good' female science with gardens." Frances Bonner, "Introduction to Sultana's Dream," in *Inventing Women: Science, Technology and Gender*, Gill Kirkup and Laurie Smith Keller, eds. (Cambridge: Polity Press, 1992), 294–302.

31. Marge Piercy, *Woman on the Edge of Time* (London: Women's Press, 1978), 105.

32. Piercy, 151.

33. Donna Haraway, "Manifesto for Cyborgs: Science, Technology and Socialist Feminism in the 1980s," in *Simians, Cyborgs, and Women,* Donna Haraway, ed. (New York: Routledge, 1991).

34. Haraway, 147.

35. Haraway, 151. In a paper delivered at St. Catherine's College, Oxford University, 30 July 1993, at a conference titled "The Uses of Knowledge: Global and Local Relations," Haraway expanded her cyborg vision to include other animal forms. She called the paper "Modest Witness @ Second Millennium. The FemaleMan Meets OncoMouse" and she argued:

> Nature and Society, animal and man: both terms collapse into each other. The great divide between Man and Nature, and its gendered corollary, that founded the story of modernity has been breached. The promises of progress, control, reason, instrumental rationality—all the promises seem to have broken in the children. The action in technoscience mixes up all the actors; miscegenation between and among the humans and the unhumans is the norm. The family is a mess. Racial purity, purity of all kinds, the great white hope of heliocentric enlightenment for a truly autochthonous Europe, the self-birthing dream of Man, the ultimate control of natural others for the good of the one—all dashed by a bastard mouse and a matched set of unmanly, fictitious humans. I find that to be highly edifying.

36. Stabile, 141.

37. Haraway, 151.

38. Fuss, 36.

39. Stabile, 13.

40. Haraway, 169.

41. Several other articles by Haraway discuss the importance of women in science. Donna Haraway, "Situated Knowledges: The Science Question in Feminism as a Site of Discourse on the Privilege of Partial Perspective," *Feminist Studies* 14, no. 3 (1988): 575–99. Donna Haraway, *Primate Visions: Gender, Race and Nature in the World of Modern Science* (New York: Routledge, 1989).

42. Arguably, Haraway's comments on the importance of controlling the agents of social construction distinguishes her from radical feminism. It was Stabile who first categorized Haraway as a technomaniac (technophile) because of her deterministic and optimistic view of technology. I agree with this interpretation of Haraway. Her emphasis upon technology compelled me to categorize her as a technophile. Also, her preoccupation with sex-based binary opposites inspires me to include her in the discussion of radical feminism.

43. Haraway, *Symians*, 150. My emphasis added.

44. Mary Anne Doane, "Commentary," in *The Signs Reader: Women, Gender and Scholarship*, Elizabeth Abel and Emily K. Abel, eds. (Chicago: University of Chicago Press, 1983), 210.

45. An unpublished paper by Colin Moran on file with the author discusses the complications of assigning medical viability due to the variety of both physical and environmental factors involved, from birthweight to neonatal facilities available. He determined that "given maximum technological aid, infants born as early as 22 weeks after conception can now survive at appreciable rates."

46. Perri Klass, "The Artificial Womb Is," *New York Times Magazine*, 29 September 1996, 116–19.

47. I further explain feminist critique of scientific experimentation and method in chapter 4 when I discuss FINRRAGE, drawing on the work of Gena Corea, Renate Duelli Klein, Robyn Rowland, Patricia Spallone, and others.

48. See Adrienne Rich and Barbara Katz Rothman as listed in the bibliography.

49. Elizabeth Spelman, *Inessential Woman* (Boston: Beacon Press, 1988), 26–27.

3

TECHNOPHOBIA: ECOFEMINISM

a gain, I return to the question, "Is technological intervention in the womb the friend or foe of women?" While the
feminists represented in the previous chapter regard technology as empowering, the feminists in this chapter are decidedly
unenthusiastic. If technophilia refers to the love of reproductive
technology as a liberating agent, technophobia refers to the fear of,
and disdain for, technological intervention in the womb.

Like technophiles, not all technophobes are feminist. For example, Jehovah's Witnesses and Christian Scientists hold purist beliefs
based on stringent concepts of life and faith. Interventions from
Cesarean section to blood transfusion to barrier methods of contraception are refused by these groups of people on grounds that are
not necessarily feminist. This chapter is concerned with *feminist* technophobes, people who are anti-technology because they believe it to
be anti-women.

Moreover, although some feminists may shun microwave ovens
and vacuum cleaners on feminist grounds, I discuss here only technophobia regarding technological intervention in the womb.

Ecofeminism

A view of radical feminism as the global equation of sex and gender
is presented in the previous chapter. However, not all radical feminists resent sexual reproduction as Firestone does. In fact, more rad-

ical feminists revere sexual difference. Susan Griffin illustrated an empowering vision of difference in 1978 in *Woman and Nature: The Roaring Inside Her.*[1] After describing how woman's essence has traditionally been constructed and subjected by patriarchy (mainly in the form of science), she then inverted this vision upon itself, presenting masculinity as otherness. She described this mission in the prologue, the only section of the book that is written in her personal voice:

> I begin the book by tracing a history of patriarchy's judgments about the nature of matter, or the nature of nature, and place these judgments side by side, chronologically, with men's opinions about the nature of women throughout history. . . . [In later chapters] the eye of patriarchy is reseen. Thus the book is not so much utopian as a description of a different way of seeing.[2]

Griffin's feminist assessment, if practically applied, might reconstruct premenstrual tension (PMT). Where PMT is deplored by nonfeminists as a sign of weakness or system failure in need of correction via medication, radical feminists celebrate a woman's special ability to communicate with herself.[3] A woman is so intricately connected with her own functions, like a spider's web, that the ripe egg tells the body it is preparing to leave the ovary by twinging muscles in the gut or lower back, by marking the face with a blemish, or through depression.

Following in the tradition of Griffin, Adrienne Rich and Barbara Katz Rothman describe their personal experiences of natural childbirth with feminist glee, celebrating labor as a catalyst and expression of feminist epiphany and power. Rothman describes her home birth:

> I never really was a "patient." I wasn't in bed; I had my contact lenses in throughout (only the myopic can understand what it means to be in touch with the world visually); I gave birth, freely and consciously—I was not *delivered.* And my baby and I were surrounded by love, not efficiency.[4]

These radical feminists redefine difference (womanhood) as a source of strength and power. In direct contrast to Firestone, Jane

Alpert argues that female biology is the source and not enemy of feminist revolution.[5] The classic hierarchy of masculine dominating feminine is inverted by asserting the value of a "feminist" femininity.

Consequently, the heading "radical feminism" represents disparate ideologies—from Firestone's woman enslaved by her body to Griffin's celebration of the female body.[6] This chapter focuses upon a particular kind of positive radical feminism: ecofeminism.[7]

Like other radical feminists, ecofeminists credit difference to essentialist or constructionist impetus. Again, it is not important to this discussion to which category of ecofeminism a particular theorist belongs, because there are central tenets to which all ecofeminists ascribe.

The fundamental creed of ecofeminism is woman's intimate connection with nature—be it innate or constructed through language, experience, and so on. Like the Earth, women are considered creative.[8] In its natural state, soil is life-giving and yielding, parallel to a woman's body:

> She opens her broad lap to him. She smiles on him. She prepares him a feast. She gives up her treasures to him. She makes him grow rich. She yields. She conceives. Her lap is fertile. Out of her dark interior, life arises.[9]

Furthermore, women resemble other life forms as we are biologically, naturally, and socially constructed parallel to animals. Griffin evokes the likeness between "great" cows and "great" women according to the patriarchal eye:

> She is a great cow. She stands in the midst of her own soft flesh, her thighs great wide arches, round columns, her hips wide enough for calving, sturdy, rounded, swaying, stupefied mass, a cradle, a waving field of nipples, her udder brushing the grass, a great cow, who thinks nothing, who waits to be milked, year after year, who delivers up calves, who stands ready for the bull, who is faithful, always there, yielding at the same hour, day after day, that warm substance, the milk white of her eye, staring, trusting, sluggish, bucolic, inert, bovine mind dozing and dreaming, who lays open her flesh, like a drone, for the use of the world.[10]

Women's creativity is not only exhibited through reproduction, but also the production of breast milk, apple pies, and clothing. Consider quilting. For centuries women have sewed intricate patterns that tell stories, celebrate occasions, decorate walls and beds, and nurture through warmth. Simply, women make things:

> Space which she embroiders. Space which she covers in quilts. Space which she makes into lace. Space which she weaves. Where she builds the house of her culture. Where her breast is a self-reflection. This space which she paints.[11]

The characterization of women as productive and creative like other animals and the land has inspired close connections between these radical feminists and the ecology movement. Ecofeminism combines respect for the natural environmental balance and the ideas of Griffin—which makes ecofeminism truly of woman born![12]

In addition to believing that there is both a spiritual and physical connection between the viability of human and non-human nature, many ecofeminists regard women as necessarily non-violent. As biological life-givers and social caretakers, women are intrinsically pacifist. Sara Ruddick developed the concept of "maternal thinking" as an important element of the peace movement.[13] She argued that character arises from, and is tested against, practice. Motherhood, the responsibility of childcare which involves protection, nurturing, and training, is work, or so-called "maternal practice." Consequently, motherhood (maternal practice) informs maternal thinking: because of what mothers do, they are necessarily nurturing people.[14] Among a compilation of essays on women and pacifism, Phylis Mack argued that although femininity has traditionally been associated with non-violence (Mahatma Gandhi is one of her examples of a pacifist attempting to lead a feminine life), maternal thinking does not preclude activism. Women can and should transport our domestic habits into the public sphere, as was demonstrated by the women of Greenham Common, who used their bodies to block the proliferation of nuclear weaponry, because militarism and force are deemed antithetical to women's essence.[15]

Consequently, ecofeminism celebrates difference, rather than lamenting it. Ecofeminists rescue femininity from the grasp of both negative radical feminists such as Firestone and patriarchal essentialists such as the Bible and Aristotle. Instead, women are esteemed unique and powerful, pure and perfect.

However, from what are women unique and different? What is the basis of comparison, the control group? Carol Stabile argues that the admiration of a female essence begs the creation of a binary masculinity:

> Claims made by [radical feminists], based as they do on spiritual or intuitive assertions, do not challenge scientific epistemologies as much as they uphold them. By asserting that women's natural, instinctive, and primal link with nature is superior to man's rational, objective, and mediated relationship to nature [or at least in opposition to man's essence], they remain trapped within the dualistic logic of rationality.[16]

The strict adherence to the idea of "woman as nature" means that all things non-woman and non-nature are necessarily the antithesis of feminine, that is, masculine. Consequently, the classic dichotomy between women and men and the character assumptions that accompany such categorization not only persist, but are vital to ecofeminism.

It is with this clear picture of these radical feminists' understanding of women that this chapter turns to a discussion of what they deem to be anti-women and what feminist technophobia might look like.

Technophobic radical feminists, like Griffin, believe that technological intervention in the womb is inherently anti-women. They advocate "the rejection of technology and the modern world in order to realign themselves with their true and essential source of strength: a pre-patriarchal affinity with nature."[17] Regardless of the specific practice or administration—imagine a woman-only clinic with pink couches, free day care, no cost for all services rendered, abundant counseling, understandable explanations of procedures and options, and free chocolate—the very idea of technological intervention in the womb is contrary to woman's essence as natural, ecological, non-violent, emotional, and holistic. Some ecofeminists declare technological intervention in the womb inherently masculine, the enemy of femininity. Why?

First, these radical feminists consider science a discourse that values the attainment of reason and objectivity as the pinnacle of human achievement. Determining the difference between man and "beast" to be cognitive thought, the craft of thinking logically is eulogized as part of the nature-culture hierarchy.[18] According to Carolyn Merchant, recognition of a mind/body dualism is the legacy of Enlightenment thinkers Descartes and Bacon.[19] These scientific philosophers sought understanding, explanation, proof, purity, and efficiency in all things—the metaphor of the machine applied to life. There are two basic elements to this rationalism: (1) the belief that all things are explicable and (2) the belief that it is indeed possible to obtain, through reason, knowledge of the nature of a given existing subject. Each of these tenets is antithetical to ecofeminism, because explanation and detachment from emotion are fundamentally hostile to the ecofeminist understanding of woman and nature. Opposed to scientific understanding and mechanical analogies, Griffin argues that women must struggle against this tendency and respect the natural balance of all things:

> I am woman born in and shaped by this civilization, with the mind of this civilization, but also with the mind and body of a woman, with human experience. Suffering grief in my own life, I have felt all the impulses that are part of my culture in my own soul. In my resistance to pain change, I have felt the will toward self-annihilation. And still the singing in my body daily returns me to a love of this earth. I know that by a slow practice, if I am to survive, I must learn to listen to this song.[20]

Thus, according to many ecofeminists, women occupy a separate sphere, a fluid existence and essential harmony that is in direct contrast to the "rational" aims of science.

The second reason ecofeminists believe technological intervention in the womb to be inherently anti-women is that in addition to valuing rationality, technological intervention values control. Underlying all scientific interference in women's bodies is the assumption that women are imperfect, and "man-made" solutions are more efficient, clean, safe, and so on: "Reproductive technology concerns itself with the control and manipulation of women's bodies; it is based on an ideological assumption that woman equals (inefficient) nature and that male medicine can do better."[21] In other words, patriarchy posits that culture is always better than nature. For example, on 9 April 1994 the *New York Times* reported that a genetically altered tomato, the "Flavr Savr," that can ripen on the vine longer before being picked for shipment had won FDA approval. In addition to enhancing vegetables, this scientific quest to improve the natural is also realized in the way that medicine seeks to colonize every aspect of reproduction.

Consider an article in the *London Times* on 28 March 1995 in which Jeremy Lawrence reported on a new technique for maintaining oxygen levels during and after birth as "A Safer Way to Be Born." Science presumes that it can improve reproduction. When technological intervention exists to prevent, create, monitor, and deliver pregnancy, is there ever a definition of women's health? Patricia Spallone argues that the scientific approach to women's bodies "would have us believe we are unable to know or control our own reproduction . . . we should always require an 'expert.' "[22] Daly is greatly concerned by the wide acceptance of the perceived necessity of external control over women's bodies:

> There is actually no natural (wild) state of femaleness that is legitimated/allowed in the Gynecological State, and this denial of female be-ing is the essence of it's gynocidal intent. There are only two possibilities. First there is a fallen state, formerly named sinful and symbolized by Eve, presently known as sick and typified in the powerless but sometimes difficult and problematic patient. Second, there is the restored/redeemed state of perfect femininity, formerly named saintly and symbolized by Mary, presently typified in the weak 'normal' woman whose normality is so elusive that it must constantly be re-enforced through regular check-ups, 'preventive medicine,' and perpetual therapy.[23]

The idea that women's bodies do not represent an ecological balance or a natural state of freedom, but an inefficient, crude, septic state of illness in need of medical attention and intervention (that is, control), is intrinsically opposed to the radical view of women as perfect, balanced, and powerful.

Third, technological intervention—what Daly describes as the Gynecological State—is fundamentally divisive. Women are not left to

function in the interconnected fashion in which our ovaries, decisions, personalities, and relationships actually operate. The Gynecological State attends to women in parts: "Medicine represents the
carving up of women's bodies in its own divisions: obstetrics, gynae-
cology, paediatrics, neonatal paediatrics, fetal medicine, reproductive medicine, have symbolically segmented women's bodies for
medical purposes."[24] The idea that the fetus is a separate entity temporarily lodging within the confines of a woman's body, or that an
egg is a commodity that can be stripped from the ovary, or that labor
can be proceeding "too slowly" such that induction is "necessary,"
is inherently anti-woman. Distinctions among parts, functions, or
time frames are irrelevant in the realm of women's perfect natural
state. Griffin describes seven men standing around a fallen tree
(which we assume they have cut down) cataloging its age, type, and
so on by slicing off branches and lodging axes into the trunk.[25] From
her description, we gather that it is no longer a tree once it is broken
into separate parts. Similarly, the division of a woman's body into
tiny parts is anti-holistic, anti-nature, and thus anti-woman.[26]

Rationality, control, and partition—the intrinsic functions of
technological intervention—often depend upon the physical use of
instruments of destruction such as knives and lasers:

> They cannot, it seems, understand nature and natural phenom-
> ena if they leave them intact with their given environment. Vio-
> lence and force are therefore intrinsic methodological
> principles of the modern concept of science and knowledge.
> They are not, as is often assumed, ethical questions which arise
> only on the application of the results of this science. They be-
> long to the epistemological and methodological foundations
> of modern science.[27]

Merchant argued that scientific method is based upon violence and
power. Because women's essence includes pacifism, these ecofeminists have identified the disruption of Mother Nature via the use of
reproductive technology as both methodologically and ideologically
violent, and therefore anti-woman.

Consequently, the fourth reason these radical feminists reject
technological intervention in the womb is that such interference
necessarily involves force. Feminists for Life often describe abortion

as "surgical rape" of women and others have utilized similar "violence against women" slogans with reference to Cesarean sections and laparoscopic surgery. Sheila Kitzinger has given several talks and even created a telephone help-line for women who have experienced violent births. Her data suggests that women use the same words and images of alienation, domination, and loss to describe both rape and bad birth experiences.[28]

Finally, pervasive scientific attention to reproduction treats women not as living, evolving, and feeling agents, but as entities of inquiry. Science, the systematized knowledge of reproduction, requires an object of study, an "other." The uniquely female activity of creating life has become a "subject" of inquiry, a scientific "project," and the colonization of this final frontier (nature) has become a "race" or "mission." Robyn Rowland argues that "there is a common belief that ideas or theories are somehow separate entities inhabiting a place called academia, remote from reality. So the scientific control of reproductive technology is often debated as if it is an intellectual exercise."[29] In the land of scientific inquiry and knowledge, women are alienated from their bodies by becoming objects of inquiry and attention. This occurs not only in the mind of the medic and of society, but also in woman's perception of her self. "The sexual objectification of woman produces a duality in feminine consciousness. . . . What occurs is not just the splitting of a person into mind and body but the splitting of the self into a number of personae, some who witness and some who are witnessed."[30]

Having explained the ecofeminist understanding of technological intervention in the womb, it is clear why these theorists can be considered technophobes: because of their strict assignment of gender, they are forced into a dualism whereby all things anti-women (unnatural) are necessarily masculine. They believe that the very idea of technological intervention in the womb is innately anti-women.[31]

Critique of Ecofeminism

There are several drawbacks to the ecofeminist approach to reproductive technology. First, claims about technology made by ecofeminists "do not challenge scientific epistemologies as much as they

51

uphold them. By asserting that women's natural, instinctive and pri-
mal link with nature is superior to man's rational, objective and me-
diated relationship to nature, they remain trapped within the
dualistic logic of rationality."[32] The idea that difference is a source
of functional meaning is not new or original. Male domination has
depended on and fomented the idea of women's difference as second-class otherness since the beginning of time. Although assessments and prescriptions vary according to certain time periods and
cultures, the idea of "femininity" has always existed, and the feminine have accordingly been subjected to second-class status in almost every historical time and place. Examine the neo-conservative
work of Phyllis Schlafly. A biological essentialist, she, too, views the
relationship between the sexes as purely and totally dualistic. However, she is not a feminist; for example, in her mind, good marriages
depend on admiring and appreciative wives who are cheerful.[33]

> Every successful country and company has one chief executive
> officer. None successfully functions with responsibility equally
> divided between cochairmen or copresidents. . . . If marriage
> is to be a successful institution, it must likewise have an ultimate
> decision-maker, and that is the husband.[34]

Note that Schlafly's eulogy of women's special role is not wholly
unlike some ecofeminists' reverence for gender-specific traits and
abilities. This close kinship between ecofeminists and neo-conserva-
tives is troublesome. "Despite the lengthy history of the hegemonic
and misogynistic uses of this connection, it is . . . perpetually redis-
covered, dressed in fashionable clothes, and presented, despite its
antiquity, as a radical new idea."[35] Although it is admirable and well
intended to re-view gender in a feminist light, "there is nothing
more difficult and dangerous, or more doubtful of success, than an
attempt to introduce a new order of things in any state."[36] In a world
where a woman earns sixty-six cents for every man's dollar, the diet
industry grosses $33 billion each year, and battering is the greatest
single cause of injury to women (more than car accidents, rapes,
and muggings combined), is it prudent for feminists to assume that
difference can be reassessed as a source of empowerment?[37] In such
a male-dominated society, it is more likely that difference will be
used to justify our oppression. In the name of political discretion,

feminists should abandon arguments that depend upon universal, inevitable, and permanent difference.

In response to this prudentialism, one might argue that it is important to advocate a politically flawed principle if the basic tenets are so pure that denying them in the name of efficacy would be unjust. However, the very postulation of a quintessential femininity by both technophiles and technophobes represents a flawed analysis of reality.

The idea that a definite gender binary exists is problematic. The concept of a single nature for all women that is universal and inevitable is flatly untrue. Sisterhood is not global. In "An Open Letter to Mary Daly," Audre Lorde confessed her frustration with essentialist feminism as white, Eurocentric, and middle-class:

> Why doesn't Mary deal with Afrekete as an example? Why are her goddess images only white, Western European, Judeo-Christian? Where was Afrekete, Yemanje, Oyo, and Mawulisa? Where were the warrior goddesses of the Vodun, the Dahomeian Amazons, and the warrior women of Dan?[38]

bell hooks, Elizabeth Spelman, Cherrie Moraga, and others have also pointed to the absence of recognition of race, class, and sexuality in most radical feminist thought.[39] If these factors are indeed significant aspects of women's lives (that is, if difference *among* women exists), then certainly biological and natural essentialists have missed something in their analysis. However, radical constructionists announce that regardless of different biological and natural factors, all women suffer oppression under patriarchy. In other words, patriarchy creates a caste of women. Yet, "to imply that all women suffer the same oppression simply because we are women is to lose sight of the many tools of patriarchy. . . . There is a pretense to the word *sisterhood* [even in its socially constructed form] that does not in fact exist."[40] Consider the following statistics regarding the unique situation of African-American women:

- Before *Roe vs. Wade*, ten thousand women died each year in the U.S. from illegal abortions, and 50 percent of these women were women of color.[41]
- In 1987–88, more white women than African-American women

were diagnosed with breast cancer, but 32 percent of African-American women as opposed to 24 percent of the white women died from it.[42]

- The average salary of an African-American female college graduate in a full-time position is less than that of a white male high-school dropout.[43]
- Forty percent of street prostitutes are women of color. Fifty-five percent of those arrested are women of color. Eighty-five percent of prostitutes sentenced to do jail time are women of color.[44]

Equating white and African-American women's experiences is at best an oversight in an attempt to reduce gender oppression to a palatable dualism, masculinity-femininity. Moreover, although less analysis exists, it is safe to assume that the experiences of Latina women and Asian-American women (broad categories in themselves) are also disparate.

The simplification of women's experiences and existence is reductionist because it ignores not only racial realities, but also the implications of sexuality, age, historical context, and so on. Even the supposedly monolithic and privileged category "white women" is extremely diverse and unpredictable. For example, white women can be harassed and abused, graduate-school educated and illiterate, living in rural, suburban, or urban areas.[45] Further, radical feminists who make sweeping assumptions about women ignore perhaps the most significant social reality, wealth. Elizabeth Grosz listed the serious problems eluding radical feminists, particularly essentialists:

> They are necessarily ahistorical; they confuse social relations with fixed attributes; they see fixed attributes as inherent limitations to social change; and they refuse to take seriously the historical and geographical differences between women—differences between women across different cultures as well as within a single culture.[46]

I do not mean to imply that the recognition of gender as an analytic category is pernicious: this would fly in the face of feminism's very existence. Rather, recognizing gender as the direct product of sexual difference (or universal oppression) and the attribution of certain attitudes and abilities to gender is not only theoretically problematic, but detrimental. Promulgation of technophobic policy (or, for that matter, technophilic policy) in the name of "women" ignores the fact that the impact of such policies will affect women disparately. As Lorde recognized, "When patriarchy dismisses us, it encourages our murderers. When radical lesbian feminist theory dismisses us, it encourages its own demise."[47]

Conclusion

Ecofeminist radical feminism should not be dismissed out of hand. Much of ecofeminism is highly compelling. There have been months when I have literally felt the passing of my egg through my cramped tummy and I have rejoiced rather than winced, celebrating this pain as a special "internal intercom system" and something only women can experience. Ecofeminism encourages young girls to rejoice at puberty and voluptuous women to revel in their curves. Ecofeminism celebrates the notion of sisterhood, like a giant slumber party. Simply, ecofeminism challenges every aspect of the social order. It has dramatically changed the way we think about the world and women's place in it. After the contributions of Griffin, Daly, and others, feminists not only ask, "Why are women not paid the same as men?" We ask, "Why is our labor valued in hourly wages?"

It is delusive and unproductive to assign binary categories to people. Sweeping assignment of an inevitable essence is unrealistic. We are not dualistic beings living in a dualistic world. Women live in the context of male oppression as multifaceted agents. We are straight, bisexual, and lesbian, Chinese and Cuban, physically disabled and abled, and wealthy and poor. A praxis feminist assessment of technological intervention in the womb must be cognizant of the social characteristics and realities of the women attached to those wombs.

Furthermore, in addition to creating universal categories of women and men, much of radical feminism treats technology as monolithic. It is the idea of technology—and science, for that matter—that these feminists confront. Although a comprehensive feminist framework is needed, it should be a set of standards against which particular technologies can be measured. Accepting or denying the mere idea of technology is as unrealistic as treating women as a ubiquitous class.

Notes

1. Of course, there were earlier references to an inverted sexual hierarchy. Carl Degler mentions several early positive radical feminist theorists in "Darwinians Confront Gender; or, There is More to It than History," in *Theoretical Perspectives on Sexual Difference*, Deborah Rhode, ed. (New Haven: Yale University Press, 1990), 33–46. Degler argues that Lester Frank Ward has been cited as the first to subscribe to a "gynocentric view" of human development. Also, Eliza Gamble and Charlotte Perkins Gilman celebrated the possibility of an improved world thanks to women's social and mental contribution.

2. Griffin, xvi.

3. Similarly, gay-rights activists took the pink triangle they were forced to wear in concentration camps during the Holocaust, turned it upside down, and made it the symbol of gay solidarity and pride.

4. Barbara Katz Rothman, *In Labor* (London: W.W. Norton, 1991), 22. See also, Adrienne Rich, *Of Woman Born: Motherhood as Experience and Institution* (New York: W.W. Norton, 1976).

5. Alpert, 91.

6. In a particularly provocative article called "Lady Love Your Cunt" appearing in *Suck* magazine (founded in summer 1969), Germaine Greer advocated masturbation, self-photography, and exercise as means of self-appreciation and celebration of the female body more generally. Reprinted in *The Madwoman's Underclothes: Essays and Original Writings*, Germaine Greer, ed. (New York: Atlantic Monthly Press, 1986).

7. In an introduction to ecofeminism appearing in *Ms.* magazine, Lindsy van Gelder wrote:

"The term 'ecofeminism' was first coined by the French writer Francoise d'Eaubonne in 1974, but it wasn't until 1980—partially in response to Three Mile Island—that Ynestra King, peace activist-writer Grace Paley, and others organized Women and Life on Earth: A Conference on Ecofeminism in the 80's at the University of Massachusetts at Amherst. The following year, the first West Coast Ecofeminism Conference was held at Sonoma State University, organized largely by people who weren't aware of the Amherst meeting."

Lindsy van Gelder, "It's not Nice to Mess with Mother Nature," *Ms.* (January/February 1989): 60–63, 62.

8. The difference between negative (Firestone) and positive radical feminists

(Griffin) is their regard for natural characteristics. The former consider the body the source of women's oppression, while the latter uphold the body and feminine essence as traits to cherish, celebrate, and utilize in the struggle for liberation.

9. Griffin, 53.

10. Griffin, 67.

11. Griffin, 169–70.

12. Excellent introductions to ecofeminism include Judith Plant, ed., *Healing the Wounds: The Promise of Ecofeminism* (Philadelphia: New Society Publishers, 1989); Karren J. Warren, ed., *Ecological Feminism* (London: Routledge, 1994); and Maria Mies and Vandana Shiva, *Ecofeminism* (London: Zed Books, 1993). For a provocative review of Mies and Shiva, see Maxine Molyneux and Deborah Lynn Steinberg, "Mies and Shiva's *Ecofeminism*: A New Testament?" *Feminist Review* (Spring 1995): 86–107.

13. Sara Ruddick, *Maternal Thinking: Toward a Politics of Peace* (New York: Ballantine Books, 1989). Virginia Woolf also attributes women's pacifism to our capacity for motherhood in *Three Guineas* (London: Hogarth Press, 1938). I thank Faith Salie for this insight.

14. Ruddick acknowledges that, according to her socialized definition of motherhood as maternal practice, men can also be mothers. (Indeed, Mack cites mostly male examples of people leading feminine peace-loving lives. See note 15.) However, in the past and present, it is overwhelmingly women who are primarily responsible for child rearing. In a time when most women are employed, it is interesting to consider the role of child minders and day care facilities as maternal, according to Ruddick's definition.

15. Phylis Mack, "Feminine Behavior and Radical Action," in *Rocking the Ship of State*, Ynestra King and Adrienne Harris, eds. (London: Westview Press, 1989). Since several of her examples of activists aspiring to maternal thinking (and practice) are men, Mack is a good example of a social constructionist ecofeminist. Again, essentialist/constructionist distinctions are not integral to this discussion. I merely mean to allude to the diversity of ecofeminism.

16. Stabile, 54.

17. Stabile, 51.

18. It should be noted that the very notion of separating man from "beast" is anti-woman, since radical feminists (especially ecofeminists) deem women to be inextricably connected with non-humans and ecological systems.

19. Carolyn Merchant, *The Death of Nature: Women, Ecology and the Scientific Revolution* (New York: Harper and Row, 1980).

20. Susan Griffin, "Split Culture," in *Healing the Wounds: The Promise of Ecofeminism*, Judith Plant, ed. (Philadelphia: New Society Publishers, 1989), 7–17, 17.

21. Robyn Rowland, *Living Laboratories* (Bloomington: Indiana University Press, 1992), 215–16.

22. Patricia Spallone, *Beyond Conception* (London: Macmillan, 1989), 103.

23. Daly, *Gyn/Ecology*, 231.

24. Rowland, 211; citing Ann Oakley, *The Captured Womb: A History of the Medical Care of Pregnant Women* (Oxford: Basil Blackwell, 1984).

25. Griffin, *Woman and Nature: The Roaring Inside Her*, 63–64.

26. Note that the divorce of a woman's body from itself lends credence to the aforementioned masculine attributes of rationality and control. Thus, the reasons why these radical feminists distrust science are interdependent.

27. Mies and Shiva, 47.

28. Sheila Kitzinger, "Birth and Violence against Women: Generating Hypotheses from Women's Accounts of Unhappiness after Childbirth," in *Women's Health Matters*, Helen Roberts, ed. (London: Routledge, 1992), 63–80.

29. Rowland, 3.

30. Sandra Lee Bartky, "Narcissism, Femininity and Alienation," *Social Theory and Practice* 8 (1987): 127–43, 138.

31. This is not to suggest that technophobes are necessarily against using technology in all aspects of reproduction. For example, not all technophobes believe that terminating pregnancy or having an emergency Cesarean section are anti-woman. However, the highly medicalized, institutionalized, and routinized form of abortion practiced in many clinics and the shockingly high rate of Cesarean section delivery in the United States would certainly be contrary to ecofeminist thought. Instead, many ecofeminists draw lines between natural and artificial control, celebrating menstrual extraction and lamenting surgical abortion, heralding the honeycap and opposing the pill. See, Inga Musico, "Abortion, Vacuum Cleaners and the Power Within," in *Listen Up: Voices from the Next Feminist Generation*, Barbara Findlen, ed. (Seattle: Seal Press, 1995), 160–66.

32. Stabile, 54.

33. Phyllis Schlafly, *The Power of the Positive Woman* (New York: Arlington House Publishers, 1977), 54–55.

34. Schlafly, 50.

35. Stabile, 53.

36. This is Machiavelli's famous description of the likelihood of becoming a successful prince without the use of force. Niccolo Machiavelli, *The Prince*, trans. Christian E. Detmold (New York: Airmont Publishing, 1965), 33.

37. Respectively: statistic based on annual earnings, U.S. Department of Labor, 1992. (See also Appendix A.) Molly O'Neill, "Congress Looking into Diet Business," *New York Times*, 28 March 1990. Coalition of Battered Women's Advocates, New York, 1992. As compiled by the Women's Action Coalition (WAC), *WAC Stats: The Facts about Women* (New York: New Press, 1993).

38. Audre Lorde, "An Open Letter to Mary Daly," in *Sister Outsider* (Trumansburg, N.Y.: Crossing Press, 1984), 66–72, 67. See also Beah Richards, "A Black

Woman Speaks," in *9 Plays by Black Women*, Margaret B. Wilkerson, ed. (New York: Mentor Books, 1986), 29–40. This one-woman performance piece, first performed in 1950 in Chicago, beautifully and forcefully decries the like oppression of black and white women.

39. Their criticism is mainly leveled at essentialist understandings of women. However, radical constructionist views that assume all women have a fixed essence are also subject to reproach as overly sweeping visions of all women. Specifically, see bell hooks, *Ain't I a Woman: Black Women and Feminism* (Boston: South End Press, 1981); Elizabeth Spelman, *Inessential Woman: Problems of Exclusion in Feminist Thought* (Boston: Beacon Press, 1988); Cherrie Moraga, *Loving in the War Years* (Boston: South End Press, 1983); Cherrie Moraga and Gloria Anzaldúa, eds., *This Bridge Called My Back: Writings by Radical Women of Color* (New York: Kitchen Table, 1983); Deborah King, "Multiple Jeopardy: The Context of a Black Feminist Ideology," in *Feminist Frameworks*, 3rd ed., Alison Jaggar and Paula Rothenberg, eds. (New York: McGraw-Hill, 1993), 220–36; Julianne Malveaux, "Gender Difference and Beyond: An Economic Perspective on Diversity and Commonality among Women," in *Theoretical Perspectives on Sexual Difference*, Deborah Rhode, ed. (New Haven: Yale University Press, 1990), 226–38.

40. Lorde, 67.

41. The Alan Guttmacher Institute, "Facts in Brief: Abortion in the United States," 1991. The information contained in footnotes 42–44 was compiled by the Women's Action Coalition (WAC).

42. Paula Ries and Anne J. Stone, eds., *The American Woman 1992–93* (New York: W.W. Norton, 1992).

43. Sara Rix, ed., *The American Woman 1990–91* (New York: W.W. Norton, 1990).

44. Frederilue, Delcoste and Priscila Alexander, eds., *Sex, Work, Writings by Women in the Sex Industry* (Cleiss Press, 1987).

45. See Catharine MacKinnon, "From Practice to Theory, or What Is a White Woman Anyway?" *Yale Journal of Law and Feminism* (1991): 13–22.

46. Grosz, 86.

47. Lorde, 69.

4

Technophobia: (FINR)Rage Against the Machine

While ecofeminists oppose the very idea of technological intervention in the womb, there is a loosely configured international group of feminists who have opposed the development and administration of many reproductive technologies for nearly two decades.

In 1979 at Hampshire College, Amherst, Massachusetts, ninety people took part in a workshop (organized and directed by Helen B. Holmes) titled, "Ethical Issues in Human Reproduction Technology: Analysis by Women." The goals of this conference were to establish dialogue among feminists concerned with new and older reproductive technologies and to discuss how to assess these entities and procedures. "Our official purpose did not include setting up an action agenda, but a surge of participant activism urged that we make specific policy recommendations while we were together, in the form of resolutions. These were created before the final session and brought to a vote on the last day."[1] The conference papers were published in two books: *Birth Control and Controlling Birth* (1980) and *The Custom-Made Child?* (1981). Most of the resolutions (which were included in the latter publication) dealt with further conferences and funding for these meetings. Yet there were also pronouncements regarding the need for an infusion of women into powerful groups and positions in pertinent medical and legislative bodies, as

61

well as brief statements on the necessity of restored Medicaid funding for abortion, the extension of prenatal care to all women, and the reduced use of fetal monitoring. Consequently, although many in attendance were proto-ecofeminists who deemed science itself inherently anti-women, this early gathering was concerned with the just organization and administration of specific technologies. The attendees were uneasy about the discriminatory distribution of resources (specifically the alienation of black and poor women due to market allocation of goods and services) and the male-dominated nature of related institutions of medicine. In the introduction to *Custom-Made Child?*, Holmes argued that the present cult of technology was characterized by the following notions: male domination, hierarchism, exploitation of nature, objectification, profit, and the belief that technology is intrinsically good.[2] Yet, while Holmes and others were troubled by the present use of technology in reproduction, they were optimistic about the possibilities for feminist reform. Holmes spends the second half of the introduction arguing that it is possible to infuse feminist values—specifically, respect for the individual, the personal as political, autonomy and choice, wholeness of the individual, wholeness of women as a community, wholeness of the future, wholeness of the ecosystem, connectedness, and non-hierarchism—into the organization and administration of reproductive technology.[3]

Five years later, this optimism waned. By 1984, despite low success rates, more than one hundred IVF teams had set up clinics advertising "treatment," surrogacy was a growing industry, access to abortion in the United States was increasingly restricted to adult women who could afford to pay for it, and the world's first IVF baby derived from a frozen and thawed embryo was delivered by Cesarean section.[4] Perhaps in response to these events, a few of the activist-authors who participated in the first conference became increasingly agitated. A handful of women decided it was necessary to approach technological intervention in the womb more seriously. They asked, "Who benefits from reproductive technology?" Rita Arditti, Renate Duelli Klein, and Shelley Minden edited a book of articles, *Test-Tube Women*, in an attempt to foster further debate on, and publicity for, this question.[5] Although the articles varied in subject matter from sterilization to in vitro fertilization to abortion, all the authors agreed that the main benefactor of the "miracle" of reproductive technology was not women, but "industry." Referring to the "capitalist takeover" of reproduction, they insisted that "reproduction was fast becoming a privileged trope for the logic of expansion and investment."[6] Reproduction was no longer a natural facet of human existence, but a business venture. *Test-Tube Women* and Gena Corea's *Mother Machine* were published in the mid-1980s and later became virtual "bibles" for FINRRAGE.

The Second International Interdisciplinary Congress on Women was held in Groningen, The Netherlands, in April 1984. Holmes organized a panel there with a focus on sex selection. It was there that Feminist International Network on the New Reproductive Technologies (FINNRET) was created, with Gena Corea, Renate D. Klein, Janice Raymond, and Robyn Rowland as the core author-activists. The panel in Groningen compiled another collaborative book of essays—*Man-Made Women: How New Reproductive Technologies Affect Women*—with nine editors alphabetized to be egalitarian.

In July 1985 the five core members felt that an "emergency" existed and organized the "Emergency" conference in Vällinge, Sweden. It was there that FINNRET became FINRRAGE (Feminist International Network of Resistance to Reproductive and Genetic Engineering). FINRRAGE held further conferences in Canada, Brussels, Australia, Austria, and Bangladesh.

One of the main purposes of the group and these frequent conferences was to publish as much anti-"infertility-treatment" material in books, magazines, newspapers, and so on as possible to heighten public awareness of the negative implications of these experiments. In 1988 FINRRAGE started an interdisciplinary journal called *Reproductive and Genetic Engineering: Journal of International Feminist Analysis.* After five years this journal could no longer be funded.

Although the original two publications following the 1979 conference identified male domination as one facet of reproductive technology, *Test-Tube Women* and subsequent books and conferences focused almost exclusively on this point. They argued that both the administration and development of reproductive technology were sites of male domination. Each of these areas deserves further attention.

With respect to the administration of reproductive technology,

FINRRAGE gave many examples of oppression. Corea has high-lighted the historically oppressive nature of the procedures of in vitro fertilization, egg collection, and hysterectomy. For example, she argues that medics prefer women to be sedated during these procedures, and her descriptions frequently include an anecdotal portrait of the woman reclined or strapped down. In between re-marks regarding the ugly truth of specific procedures, she sprinkles parables about cow reproduction, demonstrating the unpleasant similarities in care and consideration. Emphasizing the aggressive nature of the practitioners as opposed to the passive and victimized state of the woman, she notes that many eggs were stolen from wom-en's bodies:

> Women undergoing laparoscopy as part of an infertility exam or for sterilization; women undergoing hysterectomies for uter-ine fibroids or for cervical cancer or for "premalignant dis-eases;" women operated on for endometriosis and for polycystic ovaries; and women undergoing unspecified "gyne-cological surgery" in the United States and other countries have had eggs taken from their bodies.[7]

Furthermore, Corea contends that doctors who became frustrated by having to wait for ovulation before fishing for eggs gave women injections in an attempt to control not only women's body parts, but bodily processes:

> Through these powerful hormones, men controlled the ovula-tion of women. They had 'taken over the first part of the men-strual cycle of our patients,' Edwards wrote. 'Fine control has been imposed on the initiation of maturation and the timing of ovulation in cyclic women by injecting gonadotropins.' [They] assumed the role of hypothalamus. . . . Here are men taking over one function of a woman's brain.[8]

In addition to lamenting the actual procedures and attitudes of practitioners, these feminists have written at length about the lan-guage of reproductive technology. The words and phrases used rein-force the male domination of reproduction. Emily Martin wrote about the alienation of women from their selves due to the medicali-zation and institutionalization of birth. She explained that many phrases deny agency to women—such as "she delivered," "went into labor," and "gave birth"—contributing to imagery and consequent actual understanding of women as little more than machine or raw material for doctors to manipulate.[9] (Although not affiliated with FINRRAGE, Barbara Berg similarly notes that gender-biased, pejorative language is also widely used in the field of infertility. Women who have a history of spontaneous abortion are called "*habitual* aborters" and miscarriages are often attributed to an "*incompetent* cervix." Women who have trouble conceiving may be diagnosed with "*hostile* cervical mucus" or an "*inadequate* luteal phase."[10]) Moreover, Corea alleges that "some researchers speak of 'fishing for eggs' in women and others 'recruiting,' 'harvesting,' or 'capturing' them. The most vivid image in the scientific journals is that of men hunting for eggs in the bodies of women."[11] Robyn Rowland pointed out that much of this oppressive language places women in the context of nature:

> [T]hey are fields to be "harvested" for eggs. A doctor performing a laparoscopy, examining each sample taken from a woman, is seen by a reporter to be "like a miner panning for human gold." By treating women as "animal nature," medical researchers distance themselves from the humanity of women and ignore the emotional impact of their experimentation.[12]

Again, note that women's supposed connection with nature is deemed an infirmity, another example of the dangerous potential for ecofeminist notions to be co-opted and used against women.

Finally, these feminists claim reproductive technology is used to oppress women because it is not women that doctors and the state necessarily seek to aid. According to this analysis, the goal of all infertility treatment, prenatal technologies, and managed birth devices and procedures is to produce a live, healthy baby—the bigger, the better—and every live, healthy baby brings great prestige and great profit to the technodoc. IVF clinics measure their success rates by babies produced, not happy women treated:

> Risks are not even the only threat IVF poses to a woman's well-being. The innumerable manipulations of her body, and the suffering they cause her, also threaten her well-being. Yet this issue is absent from the ethical and medical literature on IVF.[13]

Thus goes the argument that the focus of the industry is to "build" and "bring forth" better babies.

While many FINRRAGE feminists contend that the *administration* of reproductive technology is anti-women (and pro-pharmacrat)[14] as demonstrated by its goals, language, and actual procedures, they also insist that even in the most woman-friendly of clinic environments, reproductive technology is anti-women because its *development* is male-dominated: "Reproductive technology is a product of the male reality. . . . The technology is male-generated and buttresses male power over women."[15] Most scientists and laboratories are populated by male majorities. Many research projects are funded by private corporations with male chief executive officers and boards of directors. Moreover, regardless of the specific inequities involved, Arditti, Klein, and Minden have argued that technologies are historically specific:

> [T]hey do not fall from heaven and . . . they are not 'neutral.' In other words, a technology is not 'objective': it carries embedded in it a vision of the world and of what is considered important and valuable for the particular society where the technology is developed.[16]

For example, consider what Corea sees as the ugly history of in vitro fertilization. Corea narrates how Edwards spent many years developing techniques (and schemes) to procure eggs with which to experiment, before striking an arrangement in 1968 with Steptoe, who provided eggs from ovaries he removed from women during gynecological operations.[17] They proceeded with experimentation on women although the number of animal species and the total number of successful live births following in vitro fertilization were extremely low: fewer than two hundred rabbits, two hundred mice and fifty rats![18] Moreover, many contraceptives were first tested on women in developing countries, like human lab rats.[19]

Not only do FINRRAGE feminists claim that the use and development of technology is male-dominated, but they allege that men conspire to control this arena. In the introduction to *Test-Tube Women*, Arditti, Klein, and Minden state:

> Why is it that men are so interested in tampering with women's reproductive biology? The question is intriguing. Why is the

old boy's network spending millions to fund research on every aspect of the *female* reproductive system (why not the male?)? How sincere is this concern to help infertile women *have* children?[20]

They identify specific enemies—owners of manufacturing companies, doctors who wield these instruments, the governments that decide which programs will be legal, funded, and so on—and argue that these various agents are actually one class of people, wealthy white men. Corea's exposition of IVF development was also an indictment of Edwards and Steptoe as individuals, and Janice Raymond's comments on surrogacy documented the significant and profitable efforts of attorney Noel Keane in promulgating the practice. Regardless of whether specific people are named or whether fingers are pointed at patriarchy in general, the point that FINR-RAGE is trying to make is that people in positions of power over women work to maintain such control.

It is important to note that although FINRRAGE's criticisms echo the sentiment of much ecofeminist thought (many FINRRAGE members are indeed ecofeminists), many FINRRAGE feminists do not oppose the idea of technological intervention in the womb itself; FINRRAGE does not advocate a blanket prohibition. For example, although some FINRRAGE members have been outspoken against RU 486,[21] many still support surgical abortion—although they are wary of the implications of available abortion coupled with amniocentesis in countries such as China and India, where female feticide is prolific. Consequently, FINRRAGE feminists embrace a framework that allows for diverse policy positions depending upon the particulars of individual technologies and the context in which they are developed and administered. Moreover, there is a diversity of views within the group.

Is this the praxis feminist framework?

Critique of FINRRAGE

To their credit, FINRRAGE members frequently point out that not all women experience oppression to the same extent or in the same fashion. Their indictment not only includes discussion of sexuality, race, and class, but is often inspired by such "double" oppression.

However, although members (more than most) consider international implications and address broad demographic concerns, FINRRAGE has been criticized for ignoring the individual preferences of women.

In 1985, Naomi Pfeffer wrote an article in *Trouble and Strife* in response to *Test-Tube Women*. She argued that FINRRAGE's assessment of technologies lacks recognition of the individual interests and experiences of infertile women themselves:

> [T]he one voice that is never heard is that of the most directly implicated: the voice of infertile women. Because of their absence, this debate appears, from the perspective of an infertile woman, to be curiously ill-informed in terms of what it is like to be infertile, socially, medically, and emotionally.[22]

Pfeffer objected to the advocacy of totalitarian policies because they are based upon theory, rather than real experience. Further, she disapproved of FINRRAGE members' characterization of women who want these technologies as desperate, coerced, or prey to false consciousness. Not only does such a description alienate many women, but it is patently false, according to Pfeffer.[23]

Pfeffer's article inspired Marge Berer's comments several months later in the same publication.[24] Agreeing with Pfeffer's condemnation of FINRRAGE members' overtheoreticism, Berer argued that, in addition to being short on experience, their arguments are void of evidence and represent little more than polemical tirades. Berer argued that such imperialistic dogma is just as dictatorial as the doctors and states whom FINRRAGE feminists declare to be the enemy of women. Thus, Berer accused FINRRAGE of being more than simply false (as Pfeffer insisted): she labeled the FINRRAGE approach, which would depend upon a great deal of state intervention and power, politically dangerous. She wrote, "To kid oneself that the state is more benevolent than science to women is politically naive and dangerous."[25] Consequently, Pfeffer and Berer's complaints regarding impracticality and overtheoreticism mirror the frustrations with radical feminism: neither approach is fully inclusive of the diversity that characterizes the category "women."

The second major problem with FINRRAGE feminists is their growing pessimism regarding the prospects for change, especially where scientific knowledge and power are concerned. A growing new field of inquiry loosely called the sociology of science has influenced their skepticism.

T. S. Kuhn's *Structure of Scientific Revolutions* published in 1962 argues that scientific revolutions cannot be explained simply by the arrival of a better theory according to simple scientific criteria.[26] He contends that there are other factors besides the development of internal logic that determine scientific inquiry, research, and theory, ultimately arguing against the autonomy of science.[27] Noting that science may in fact be relative—nothing but the expression of particular interests—feminist epistemologies are apt to point out the patriarchy intimately intertwined in scientific methodology and analysis.

Unlike the optimism displayed by individuals at the 1979 initial conference, FINRRAGE members seem skeptical about the feminist possibilities for reproductive technology. Arditti, Klein, and Minden explicitly denounce the infusion of more women into science.

> [We don't] advocate 'feminist scientists' to take an active part in developing reproductive technologies: perhaps because we feel that at this point such an attempt would be a contradiction in terms. Science, we believe, mirrors the power relations in society, and to try to add feminist values to its current structure could only result in a superficial, if any, change.[28]

And Klein argues against any attempt to appropriate these technologies:

> The issue is not only who controls the new reproductive technologies, but that the technologies in themselves are invasive and destructive. Some (including some feminists) believe this reproductive technology should not be rejected out of hand. On the contrary, we should try to appropriate it. But where else are women in control of technology? . . . [T]echnologies are not neutral. . . . [I associate them] with even more loss of freedom for women, and with more bodily and spiritual damage.[29]

Raymond echoed this sentiment, arguing that regulation of technologies "functions as quality control rather than as actual challenge."[30] She insists that regulation is exactly what the developers and practitioners of reproductive technology want, because it gives them legitimacy. Thus, some FINRRAGE members conclude that, short of a complete feminist social revolution, the only feminist approach to technological intervention in the womb is abolition. Consider Klein's call to action:

> We should offer energetic resistance, prepare our own laws, determine to file legal actions against the technodocs and the pharmacrats, and against the hospitals, clinics or other institutions in which these experiments and surgical operations are carried out on our bodies. And, who knows, perhaps we should even throw a few more stink-bombs. The least we can do is to expose the techno-patriarchal bias of the new reproductive technologies and genetic engineering, and refuse to enter the dialogue on the terms of the technodocs and the clones. We should not forget that women hold one enormous power: techno-patriarchy still needs access to our bodies in order to pursue IVF and embryo research. We can capitalise on this power, refuse them access, and organize—infertile and fertile women together or separate—to fight back and resist becoming test tube women.[31]

Although their condemnation of current scientific theory and practice is extremely compelling, and any feminist response to technological intervention in the womb should incorporate many of their criticisms, must science be *permanently* patriarchal? Must feminists denounce science forever?

Evelyn Fox Keller believes in the possibility of a gender-free science populated by androgynous individuals—people capable of combining masculine and feminine characteristics—which she described in her biography of the Nobel prize-winning geneticist Barbara McClintock.[32] While most feminists are not as optimistic about the possibility of a gender-neutral science, Hilary Rose, Helen Longino, Sandra Harding, Marilyn Strathren, and others argue that under certain conditions "feminist science" is indeed possible. This optimistic social constructionist view of women and science is discussed in *Inventing Women: Science, Technology and Gender*, edited by Gill Kirkup and Laurie Smith Keller.[33] Sandra Harding's contribution focuses on the need for more women and women's values in science. Many feminists detail specific means of increasing women's numbers and presence in science, most notably Liz Whitelegg, who laments the state of scientific education for girls, and the American Association of University Women (AAUW), which advocates gender justice in the classroom. Nancy Hartsock and Hilary Rose call for the inclusion of women's experiences as scientific evidence.

Two other feminist publications that are hopeful about the potential for science to be reformed provide significant insight into the importance of women as medical research subjects. Margrit Eichler and Jeanne Lapointe wrote a short paper published by the Social Sciences and Humanities Research Council of Canada in 1985 called, "On the Treatment of the Sexes in Research." They conclude:

> Since the social situations of women and men are different, it is impossible to generalize from observations about one sex without testing whether they apply to both. Awareness of sex as a social variable therefore implies a dual perspective in research, a duality which must be reflected in appropriate language [and methods].[34]

And Sue Rosser argues in *Women's Health—Missing from U.S. Medicine* that research is androcentric, as women are excluded from trials. She believes that such shallow methodology is felt most by marginalized women—women of color, lesbians, and the elderly—and she argues that there is a great need for reform in medical school education.[35]

Consequently, these feminists demand a woman-friendly science that responds to the reality of women's experiences, much like the requests of Pfeffer and Berer. Their policy suggestions seem not only reasonable, but also hopeful. If we accept Pfeffer and Berer's contentions that some women want these technologies, isn't it more reasonable to find woman-friendly ways to accommodate these individual women's desires rather than deny them?

Conclusion

The two frustrations with FINRRAGE really involve the same quandary: although their attention to the development and administration of particular technologies is important and provocative, their more recent policy suggestions seem impractical. Ignoring some women's preferences—or discrediting them as false consciousness—and denying the possibility of feminist reform of science involves sweeping analysis. I seek a praxis feminism that will respect our diversity and radiate viable policy solutions to current injustice.

Frustrations with technophilia, ecofeminist technophobia, and FINRRAGE are interconnected. Notice that all three of the approaches to women's liberation and the role of technological intervention in the womb in our struggle place demands upon women; the locus of action and responsibility lies with women. Despite our diversity, we are told to embrace technology or reject technology or reject only certain technologies in the name of our supposed common essence or, at least, a common social position. If the freedom of women to select individual life paths—and divergent technological options—is to be respected as a realistic inevitability of our diversity, a praxis-oriented feminism must honor our wide demographics and preferences and place the onus elsewhere.

Notes

1. "Appendix: Resolutions," in *The Custom-Made Child?*, Helen B. Holmes, Betty B. Hoskins, and Michael Gross, eds. (Clifton, N.J.: Humana Press, 1981), 311.

2. Helen B. Holmes, "The Birth of Women-Centered Analysis," in *The Custom-Made Child?*, Helen B. Holmes, Betty B. Hoskins, and Michael Gross, eds. (Clifton, N.J.: Humana Press, 1981), 1–18, 3–7.

3. Holmes, 8–13.

4. Also, the very public resignation of Dr. Robyn Rowland from chairing the Committee to Coordinate the Social and Psychological Research in the New Reproductive Technologies in Melbourne, Australia (because the Queen Victoria Hospital announced its intention to introduce embryo "flushing"), sparked a national inquiry, public funding debates, and much press coverage. Renate Klein, "Genetic and Reproductive Engineering—the Global View," in *The Baby Machine*, Jocelynne Scutt, ed. (London: Green Print, 1990), 235–73, 251.

5. Betty Hoskins, Helen B. Holmes, Janice Raymond, and Ruth Hubbard are each published in both publications.

6. Jose Van Dyck, *Manufacturing Babies and Public Consent: Debating the New Reproductive Technologies* (London: Macmillan, 1995), 90. I found an interview with Jalna Hanmer in England and correspondence from Becky Holmes extremely useful in

establishing an accurate history of FINRRAGE. See also prologue to Patricia Spallone and Deborah Lynn Steinberg, eds., *Made to Order: The Myth of Reproductive and Genetic Progress* (Oxford: Pergamon, 1987).

7. Gena Corea, *The Mother Machine* (London: The Women's Press, 1985), 101.

8. Corea, 110.

9. Emily Martin, *The Woman in the Body: A Cultural Analysis of Reproduction* (Boston: Beacon Press, 1987).

10. Barbara Berg, "Listening to the Voices of the Infertile," *Reproduction, Ethics, and the Law,* Joan Callahan, ed. (Bloomington: Indiana University Press, 1995), 80–108, 101.

11. Corea, 103.

12. Robyn Rowland, "Decoding Reprospeak," *Ms.* (May/June 1991): 38–41, 38.

13. Corea, 178.

14. Pharmacrat and technodoc are derogatory words coined by Corea to describe the medics, lawyers, and businessmen who control and profit from the reproductive technology industry.

15. Corea, 4.

16. Rita Arditti, Renate Duelli Klein, and Shelley Minden, eds. *Test-Tube Women* (London: Pandora Press, 1984), xii.

17. Corea, 100–13.

18. Corea, 113.

19. Raymond writes:

> The pill was tested on women in Puerto Rico. The Dalkon Shield, taken off the market in most First World countries, remains implanted in many Third World women. Women in Brazil and Jamaica were among the first tested in Norplant trials. . . . Nevertheless, few discussions of technological reproduction and surrogacy in the West make note of the insidious growth of reproductive trafficking: the international medical research networks; the technology transfers; the global markets for surrogacy; the expanding exchange of human material from one woman to another; the increasing market for fetal tissue, eggs, and embryos for medical research; the international stockpiling of frozen embryos.

Janice Raymond, "International Traffic in Reproduction," *Ms.* (May/June 1991): 29–32.

20. Arditti et al., 2.

21. Janice Raymond, Renate Klein, and Lynette Dumble, "RU 486 No," *Ms.* (March/April 1993): 34–37.

22. Naomi Pfeffer, "Not So New Technologies," *Trouble and Strife* (Spring 1985): 46–50, 46.

23. These points were reiterated and her own experience discussed further in Naomi Pfeffer, *The Stork and the Syringe* (Cambridge: Polity Press, 1993).

24. Marge Berer, "Breeding Conspiracies: Feminism and the New Reproductive Technologies," *Trouble and Strife* (Summer 1986): 29–35.

25. Berer, 33.

26. T. S. Kuhn, *The Structure of Scientific Revolutions* (Chicago: University of Chicago Press, 1962).

27. Evelyn Fox Keller, *Reflections on Gender and Science* (New Haven: Yale University Press, 1985), 4–5 (discussing Kuhn).

28. Arditti et al., 4.

29. Klein, "Genetic and Reproductive Engineering," in *The Baby Machine: Reproductive Technology and the Commercialisation of Motherhood*, Jocelynne A. Scutt, ed. (London: Green Print, 1990), 245. Notice that much of Klein's rhetoric is reminiscent of ecofeminist sentiment. Many FINRRAGE feminists demonstrate ecofeminist tendencies, and policy commonalities exist.

30. Janice Raymond, *Women as Wombs* (New York: Harper Collins, 1993), 205.

31. Klein, "Genetic and Reproductive Engineering," 268–269.

32. Evelyn Fox Keller, *A Feeling for the Organism: The Life and Work of Barbara McClintock* (San Francisco: W. H. Freeman, 1983).

33. Gill Kirkup and Laurie Smith Keller, eds., *Inventing Women: Science, Technology and Gender* (Cambridge: Polity Press, 1992).

34. Margrit Eichler and Jeanne Lapointe, *On the Treatment of the Sexes in Research* (Ottawa: The Social Sciences and Humanities Research Council of Canada, 1985), 5.

35. Sue Rosser, *Women's Health—Missing from U.S. Medicine* (Bloomington: Indiana University Press, 1994). Also a letter to the editor appearing in the *New York Times* on 11 October 1996 excoriated the gender bias in science. Christopher Bodkin of Islip, Long Island, New York, wrote:

> The 1996 Nobel Prizes have all been announced and, as usual, not one woman has received an award in science. Since the award was established in 1901, more than 300 men and only 9 women have been honored in science. But numbers do not tell the whole story. While a student at Cambridge University, Professor Jocelyn Bell discovered pulsars, the starts that emit radio waves; the committee gave the prize to her male professors. Lise Meitner worked with Otto Hahn on fission and the physics of chain reactions, but Hahn received the prize.

Although this indictment of the scientific academy demonstrates grave gender disparity, surely it can (and should) be rectified, and this bias is not innate.

5

MY BODY, MY RIGHT

$\mathcal{N}$ early one million people marched on Washington in spring 1992, many of them carrying signs with big bold letters proclaiming, "My body, my right!" or "Keep your laws off my body!" I saw one poster announcing, "Elvis fan for choice!" and my own parents and sister carried a huge sign that read, "Family for choice!" Most of the demands centered around the creation or protection of rights—to bodily integrity, reproductive freedom, procreative autonomy—that is, entitlements as members of society.[1]

This chapter describes the status-quo approach to reproductive technology, so-called "pro-choice" feminism, as delivered by the Supreme Court and advocated by privacy feminists.

The Constitutional Right to Privacy

Evolution of Roe v. Wade

There is no specifically enumerated "right to privacy" or bodily integrity or procreative liberty or even women's equality explicitly in the American Constitution or Bill of Rights. However, as feminist legal champion Ruth Bader Ginsburg testified before the Senate in her nomination hearing to become an associate member of the U.S. Supreme Court, the Constitution is an evolving document:

> The Framers are shortchanged if we view them as having a limited view of rights, because they wrote, Thomas Jefferson wrote, 'We hold these truths to be self evident, that all men are cre-

ated equal, that they are endowed by their Creator with certain inalienable rights, that among these'—*among these*—'are life, liberty, and the pursuit of happiness, and that Government is formed to protect and secure those rights.'[2]

Indeed, many feminists believe in the existence of unenumerated rights; however, defining the scope of these rights is a challenge involving great debate.[3]

Webster's Seventh Collegiate Dictionary defines privacy as "the quality or state of being apart from company or observation: seclusion."[4] With reference to the legal codification of privacy, David Garrow argues that the first suggestions of a "right to privacy" occurred before the turn of the century. In 1888, Thomas Cooley wrote about the "right to be let alone," followed two years later by E. L. Godkin's article in *Scribner's Magazine* in which he called for a " 'right to privacy' in the context of criticizing personally salacious and intrusive newspaper reporting."[5] However, it was an article in the *Harvard Law Review* written by then-Boston lawyers Samuel D. Warren and Louis D. Brandeis that is most often cited as the original source of the idea of the right to privacy in U. S. law. They advocated recognition of protection for "the private life, habits, acts, and relations of an individual."[6]

It was not until 1965 that a right to privacy as bodily integrity was first affirmed by the Supreme Court. A Connecticut law had made it a crime to "use, advise, or abet the use of any drug, medicinal article or instrument for the purpose of preventing conception." In *Griswold v. Connecticut*, which established the right of married couples to use contraception, Justice William O. Douglas described a right to privacy in the "penumbras" of the First, Third, Fourth, and Fifth Amendments.[7]

In the decade that followed *Griswold*, many state and Supreme Court cases edged closer to the establishment of a right to privacy for unmarried people as well.[8] Although several lawyers and lawmakers in states such as New York, Arizona, and California pushed for such universal acceptance, a right to privacy for all individuals was not secured on a national level until the famous *Roe v. Wade* decision was delivered on January 22, 1973.[9] Many feminists celebrated on that day. They believed that this recognition of abortion under the auspices of a right to privacy would yield respect for the body as owned by the individual, thus allowing a woman to be the judge of all things entering and leaving her domain. However, the *Roe* decision contained two important holdings—an explanation of fetal development and a definition of the right to privacy—and neither has served to absolutely affirm a woman's right to bodily integrity as these feminists once hoped.

The status of the fetus in Roe and beyond

Writing the majority opinion, Justice Harry Blackmun devised a trimester time frame for fetal development that largely symbolized a compromise between vying scientific, religious, and feminist definitions of life. He alleged that as the fetus gained increased potential for viability, it accrued respect and protection, which would be balanced against the woman's right to privacy:

> The pregnant woman cannot be isolated in her privacy. She carries an embryo and, later, a fetus. . . . It is reasonable and appropriate for a state to decide that at some point in time another interest, that of the health of the mother or the potential human life, becomes significantly involved. The woman's privacy is no longer sole and any right of privacy she possesses must be measured accordingly. . . . Appellant and some amici argue that the woman's right is absolute. . . . With this we do not agree. . . . The Court's decisions recognizing a right of privacy also acknowledge that some state regulation in areas protected by that right is appropriate . . . a state may properly assert important interests in safe-guarding health, in maintaining medical standards, and in protecting potential life. At some point in pregnancy, these respective interests become sufficiently compelling to sustain regulation of the factors that govern the abortion decision.[10]

To determine when the state's interest becomes compelling, Blackmun created the trimester approach to govern the balancing of individual liberty and state interest.

> *Roe* established a trimester framework to govern abortion regulations. Under this rigid construct, almost no regulation at all is

permitted during the first trimester of pregnancy; regulations designed to protect the woman's health, but not to further the state's interest in potential life, are permitted during the second trimester; and during the third trimester, when the fetus is viable, prohibitions are permitted provided the life or health of the mother is not at stake.[11]

Consequently, potential human life developing within the womb of a woman's body was given a trifurcated degree of recognition that increased over time, though always falling short of legal personhood. At the point of viability, the fetus becomes a recognizable state interest and restrictions are warranted. As a result, third-trimester abortions have been seriously restricted in every U.S. state and territory, except in cases where the woman's life or health is in danger.

In 1992, the trimester approach to fetal protection was muddled, if not completely nullified, in *Planned Parenthood v. Casey*. In "exercising its reasoned judgment in determining the boundaries between the individual's liberty and the demands of organized society,"[12] the *Casey* decision reaffirmed the essential holding of *Roe*; the right to privacy covers the right to determine whether to bear or beget children, including the right to terminate pregnancy. However, the Supreme Court "rejected" the trimester framework, instead endorsing a viability standard necessarily dependent upon technological invention.[13] Writing the plurality opinion, Justice O'Connor held that "whenever viability occurs . . . it marks the earliest point at which the state's interest in fetal life is constitutionally adequate to justify a legislative ban on nontherapeutic abortions."[14] Moreover, the Supreme Court acknowledged that if technological invention once could support a twenty-eight-week-old fetus and might now support a fetus at twenty-four weeks, it is possible that viability will eventually someday be medically defined at an even earlier point in pregnancy:

> Whenever it may occur, the attainment of fetal viability may continue to serve as the critical fact, just as it has done since *Roe* was decided; which is to say that no change in *Roe*'s factual underpinning has left its central holding obsolete, and none supports an argument overruling it.[15]

More significant and novel than reaffirming the essential tenets of *Roe*, *Casey* established a new standard of judicial review with respect to privacy that gave the fetus increased protection as a state interest. Simply, not all rights in the United States accrue the same respect. According to *Roe* and subsequent cases until *Casey*, privacy was a fundamental right that was accorded strict scrutiny review: to infringe upon this liberty, a state must have compelling reasons. However, *Casey* lessened this standard of review and explicitly established an "undue burden" standard.

> To protect the central right recognized by *Roe* while at the same time accommodating the State's profound interest in potential life, the undue burden standard should be employed. An undue burden exists, and therefore a provision of law is valid, if its purpose or effect is to place substantial obstacles in the path of a woman seeking an abortion before the fetus attains viability.[16]

Reproductive privacy is no longer a fundamental right to be infringed only when the state can show a compelling interest; it is now a constitutional liberty, protected to the extent that infringements are deemed insubstantial. In *Casey*, the Supreme Court upheld Pennsylvania's provision that women must wait twenty-four hours between the provision of the information deemed necessary for informed consent and the performance of an abortion (a so-called twenty-four-hour waiting period law). Although O'Connor's opinion found the impact of these laws on women troublesome and even discriminatory (since women working outside the home and women who live far away from clinics face greater obstacles than others), regardless, she held that the twenty-four-hour waiting period did not pose an undue burden.[17] Consequently, this new standard of reviewing laws that regulate technological intervention in the womb seems quite lax.

Because O'Connor appears to be keenly aware of the serious implications of "bodily integrity" and "personal autonomy" to a woman's life and destiny, the significance of *Casey* has been initially slight—especially since many feared that the Supreme Court would overturn *Roe* completely, as Justice Scalia and Chief Justice Rehnquist urge in their dissents.[18]

It is possible that this undue-burden standard will be applied to other technological interventions in the womb, perhaps emphasizing an "adversarial approach" to pregnancy. "Adversarial policies approach the woman and the fetus she carries as distinct legal entities having adverse interests, and assume that the government's role is to protect the fetus from the woman."[19]

By not recognizing the woman as her body, no matter what the state of any organ or function within her, the state has been able to force women to use certain reproductive technologies in the name of the state's "important and legitimate interest in protecting the potentiality of human life."[20] In *Abortion & Dialogue*, Ruth Colker narrates several moving stories of women whose autonomy was trumped by the state's compelling interest in the fetuses they carried. For example, Santiago X was a pregnant Jehovah's Witness who was forced to have a blood transfusion because it was deemed necessary to save the life of a fetus.[21] Stacey Paddock was forced to have a blood transfusion during delivery.[22] In eleven states, women in childbirth have experienced "forced" technological intervention in the womb in the form of court-ordered Cesarean sections.[23] In addition to compelling technological intervention in the womb, under the auspices of the adversarial approach, women have been charged with prenatal neglect and homicide; women have been imprisoned and civilly committed for the duration of their pregnancies; women have been restricted and penalized for taking prescription drugs.[24] In Wyoming, a pregnant woman who sought medical attention at a hospital after being badly beaten by her husband was arrested while still in the emergency room and charged with endangering her fetus by drinking alcohol during her pregnancy.[25] On September 18, 1996, a circuit court Judge in Wisconsin ruled that a woman who consumed alcohol during her pregnancy must stand trial for attempted first-degree intentional homicide and reckless conduct in *State of Wisconsin v. Zimmerman*.[26] It is as if being pregnant diminishes a woman's citizenship making her subservient to that which grows in her own womb:

Does the pregnant woman have the right to exist in a vacuum with the full complement of her liberties protected, or does she, by virtue of her pregnancy, move into another class of citizen—a citizen whose obligations are such that her rights and liberties become secondary, or at least, temporarily suspended?[27]

In addition to the fact that the state has recognized the viable fetus as a separate entity within the private realm of a woman's body, the medical profession has likewise identified the fetus as a second patient housed in the woman's womb. It is doctors and hospitals who decide that an intervention is "necessary" and then petition the courts for orders of temporary custodianship.[28] Further, it is doctors and nurses who often report incidents of "fetal abuse" to the authorities.

With the advent of prenatal technologies, especially visual technologies, the state and medical profession have increasingly cherished fetal personhood. Visual representation of the development of a fetus has inspired earlier recognition of viability, contributing to a surge of restrictive abortion bills and laws.[29] Ultrasound, a device that projects an image of a free-floating fetus onto a computer screen, abets the notion that the fetus is a separate potential life deserving rights and protection. Furthermore, the proliferation of infertility treatment has meant increased reverence for the fetus. "Success" of infertility treatment is measured by the production and survival to term of a fetus, as opposed to the woman's health, happiness, or other interests. When women spend months or even years trying to conceive, the product of their efforts becomes increasingly valued as an entity worthy of respect and protection. Family photo albums often contain pictures of the petri dish and the first ultrasound.

Consider the fetal focus of childbirth. When a baby is born the doctor will typically announce its gender, weight, and length—and then occasionally, almost as an afterthought, someone will inquire about the condition of the mother, and the doctor characteristically will respond, "and the mother is doing just fine."

Focus on the fetus as a separate convalescent "burdens the pregnant woman with a duty to save fetal life at enormous cost to herself—a cost that, as a society, we ask of no man, not even the parent of a child"[30]: "Although competent adults are at liberty to refuse medical treatment, pregnant women in the United States of

America suspend their rights and are required to subsume their identity, will, and bodily integrity."[31] Consequently, these technologies have meant the further development of a distinction, even opposition, between woman and fetus, and consequently, increasing medical and state intervention.[32]

If legal fetal viability is the mere codification of scientific invention, then scientists are largely responsible for establishing the limitations of women's privacy.[33] I do not mean to imply that ultrasound is wholly responsible for reducing women's bodily autonomy. Rather, it is the Supreme Court's respect for science more generally and the use of viability as the boundary of women's autonomy that are problematic. Supreme Court Justice Sandra Day O'Connor remarked in *Akron v. Akron Center for Reproductive Health* (1983) that medical progress has put *Roe* on a collision course with itself.

> The problem is not the rolling back of *Roe*. Ironically, the very structure of the decision has opened the door to state regulation of women's bodies and lives. . . . In founding a right to privacy, the Court in *Roe* also claimed that the state had an important and legitimate interest in protecting the potentiality of human life.[34]

Moreover, since O'Connor's restatement of the significance of fetal viability in the *Casey* decision replaced the trimester approach, the scope of the adversarial model of pregnancy may be potentially expanded; the earlier viability is determined, the less privacy a woman has.

Against this dictum, privacy advocates such as Kathryn Kolbert, vice president of the Center for Reproductive Law and Policy,[35] argue that there should be a difference between the medical and (socio)legal definitions of viable life. Regardless of when doctors and scientists determine the fetus to be viable, the courts should not recognize even the potential existence of personhood within the confines of a woman's body. The integrity of the body as property should be respected by the state (and medics), regardless of the development of any organ inside it because of the acceptance of privacy as a right, an indefeasible liberty. In other words, the Supreme Court should nullify or ignore the fetal viability clause, the concept of trimester development, and the undue burden standard in favor of a strictly respected right to personal autonomy. Pregnant women's bodily integrity would then be awarded sanctity twenty-four hours a day, 365 days a year, regardless of reproductive condition. The right to privacy would be granted to all individuals indiscriminately and indefeasibly.

However, even if legal "life" was determined to begin at birth and privacy was accorded strict scrutiny regardless of reproductive condition, the constitutional definition of privacy itself is not a feminist fantasy.

The constitutional right to privacy

The constitutional right to privacy is best described as a negative right or the blocking of government curtailment. "The liberty-based right to privacy includes the right to be free from unwarranted governmental intrusion into matters so fundamentally affecting a person as the decision whether or not to bear or beget a child."[36] Thus, individual autonomy is the freedom to be left in peace. Applying this notion of constitutional privacy to reproductive technology, the Supreme Court has said that while the government cannot interfere with a woman's right to control her own reproductive organs, it does not have to decree affirmative policies that would establish such control in effect. In other words, allowing a woman's right to abortion, IVF, or anesthesia without government interference is guaranteed by the right to privacy, but the state does not have to provide those things. Rather than aiding women in acquiring such services, all people—women and men, pregnant and non-pregnant—must simply be regarded in the same "free" manner. Thus, privacy is said to abide by a "neutrality principle." All reproductive technologies are legal and available, but the state does not have the responsibility of providing any of these services or facilities to women.[37] Kolbert argues that although the government currently funds childbirth and not abortion, these two reproductive choices should be accorded even concern.

As these courts have recognized, a pregnant woman has only two ways of exercising her constitutional right of reproductive choice—she may carry to term or she may terminate the pregnancy. For a woman too poor to afford appropriate medical care, the state's offer of subsidies for one option but not the other necessarily pressures women to forgo their constitutional right of reproductive choice.[38]

Although Kolbert posits an eloquent argument for improved access to services for poor women, in fact, *Roe* has not been used to provide access for women. The neutrality principle has been interpreted to favor the equal *freedom* of individuals, as privacy is something that must be respected in all individuals, but not allocated to anyone.

While this chapter focuses largely on the right to privacy approach with respect to abortion, this constitutional reasoning also guides other technological interventions in the womb. Indeed, "procreative liberty" has been determined to be an integral element of the "right to privacy." The idea of procreative liberty was first deliberated in the United States in the *Skinner v. Oklahoma* decision in 1942.[39] Skinner challenged an Oklahoma law that mandated the sterilization of individuals who were convicted of larceny three times. (His three predicate felonies included two armed robberies and one count of stealing chickens.) Although the case mainly focused upon the unequal treatment of felons, since those convicted of embezzlement were not subject to sterilization, the Supreme Court did address the nature of sterilization itself. Recognizing that compulsory sterilization inhibited one's reproductive capacities, Justice William O. Douglas specifically referred to a right not to have one's procreative capacities interfered with: "[The statute] touches a sensitive and important area of human rights. Oklahoma deprives certain individuals of a right which is basic to the perpetuation of a race—the right to have offspring."[40] Moreover, he referred to this right as one of "the most basic civil rights of man."[41] As Athena Liu notes, "*Skinner* has often been considered the milestone in claims that it is appropriate to discuss procreation in terms of human rights."[42]

In addition to *Skinner*, the Supreme Court's protection of an individual's right not to reproduce (in *Griswold*, *Eisenstadt*, and *Roe*) has been correlatively interpreted to mean that individuals have a right to reproduce.

The right to be a parent or not has most notably been applied to conceptive technologies and assisted pregnancy. Though not a feminist, John Robertson champions the right to procreation as informing the legality of all reproductive technologies. In his book, *Children of Choice: Freedom and the New Reproductive Technologies*, he argues for access to several technological interventions in the womb under the auspices of the "freedom to decide whether or not to have offspring and to control the use of one's reproductive capacity":[43]

> Claiming that procreative liberty is grounded in the U.S. Constitution, Robertson has popularized the concept and has been the chief legal missionary for promoting reproductive technologies and contracts based on this principle. . . . Procreative liberty, in fact, has become a slogan of the new reproductive technologies establishment in much the same way that sexual freedom became the buzzword of the sexual liberation movement of the sixties.[44]

One example of a procreative liberty defended by some privacy feminists is surrogacy.[45] In the 1980s America became familiar with these contractual arrangements when Marybeth Whitehead, impregnated through alternative insemination with the sperm of William Stern, decided to keep the child she contributed an egg to and carried to term. Judge Harvey Sorkow, who presided over the "Baby M" trial, ruled in favor of Stern's right to contract a woman's womb as merely exercising the right to procreate by using alternative assistance.[46] Thus, Sorkow affirmed the position of Robertson and others who believe in procreative liberty:

> It must be reasoned that if one has a right to procreate coitally, then one has a right to reproduce non-coitally. If it is the reproduction that is protected, then the means of reproduction are also protected . . . this court holds that the protected means extends to the use of surrogates.[47]

Judge Sorkow was overruled by the New Jersey Supreme Court, which invalidated the contract as conflicting with the law and public policy of the state that prohibited baby-selling, since Baby M was Whitehead's genetic daughter.[48] However, gestational surrogacy contracts (where the surrogate contributes her "services" but not her egg) have been held constitutional on privacy grounds, most recently in California in *Johnson v. Calvert.*

Mark and Crispina Calvert were a married couple who wanted to have a genetic child. Although Crispina had undergone a hysterectomy five years earlier, her ovaries remained capable of egg production. The Calverts contracted Anna Johnson to carry their embryo to term for the sum of ten thousand dollars, the last installment to be paid after the child's birth. Relations between the parties deteriorated, and the Calverts and Anna Johnson each filed for a declaration of parenthood. The New Jersey Court distinguished this purely gestational case from *In re Baby M* on the basis that Whitehead contributed an egg and was genetically related to the child the contract purported to "sell." The court held that gestational surrogacy contracts do not violate adoption statutes, prohibitions of involuntary servitude, or public policy concerns that such contracts may exploit or dehumanize women, especially low-income women. Moreover, the court decided that enforcement of surrogacy arrangements is not an affront to the birth mother's right to privacy and procreative freedom:

> Women who entered into gestational surrogacy arrangements did not have any right of privacy requiring recognition and protection of her status as "birth mother"; such a woman was not exercising her own right to make procreative choices but was agreeing to provide necessary and important service without any expectation that she would raise the child on her own.[49]

Citing the work of Robertson as well as both Carmel Shalev and Marjorie Shultz,[50] the California Court held that in surrogacy arrangements it is the contracting couple who are exercising their right to procreative liberty: "Gestational surrogacy, like the other reproductive technologies that extend the ability to procreate to persons who might not otherwise be able to have children, enhances individual freedom, fulfillment and responsibility."[51]

Critique of the constitutional approach to privacy and procreative liberty

There are several reasons why I believe that the constitutional definition of privacy that endorses state abstention is a facile feminist approach.

means used to bring about the desired end. Procreative liberty is not an abstract end, separate from an evaluation of the means. The central fact is that women's bodies are the reproductive means to others' reproductive goals.[65]

What are the ramifications of referring to women as reproductive servants or the channel of another's right to reproduce? As the means of fulfilling another's right to procreative liberty, the womb may become a commodity for consumption, and control of this entity may be shared by many actors, rather than by the woman who is her body. Contracting agents may be able to exert decision-making power over women's bodies in the name of satisfying their right to reproduce, claiming the "free" participation of women as justification. The most dramatic example of the pregnant woman's loss of self as a conduit of another's liberty interest is the instance of postmortem ventilation (PMV). This involves pregnant brain-dead women who are "kept alive" by artificial means until the fetus is strong enough to be extracted. Following delivery, the woman is left to expire naturally. Consider the exploitation of Donna Piazzi. She was sixteen weeks pregnant when she was found unconscious and not breathing on the floor of a public restroom. (Note that sixteen weeks is well before the point of fetal viability.) Emergency medical personnel used machines to resuscitate her breathing and heartbeat, though she was pronounced "brain-dead." After three weeks of this lifeless condition, her husband asked that the physicians disconnect her respirator and cease intravenous feedings, allowing her to expire naturally. However, another man, the undisputed biological father of the fetus, opposed this request. He wanted to keep her ventilated so that "his" fetus could develop within her. The hospital successfully sought declaratory judgment to permit PMV in the interests of the biological father and the (non-viable) fetus. It is possible that many women would prefer this treatment. However, without any understanding or inquiry regarding her desires (and contrary to the wishes of her next of kin), Donna Piazzi's body was literally used as a human incubator.[66] Although the Supreme Court has yet to rule on the constitutionality of PMV, these situations will now be assessed according to the undue burden standard and it is even more likely that these brain-dead women will be ventilated for the benefit of another.

When wombs can be rented and eggs purchased, the woman who creates and labors over these commodities is viewed merely as shopkeeper or owner, rather than as a complete human being. In surrogate arrangements, the woman is little more than a conduit for another's right to reproduce. The contractors may request certain dietary or exercise arrangements or even request Cesarean section delivery in the name of protecting their right to reproduce.[67] Women become baby machines.[68]

However, privacy feminists such as Laura M. Purdy and Carmel Shalev claim that women who participate in surrogate agreements or egg-donor programs consent to these legal arrangements and these contracts are binding civil agreements since it is assumed that participation is willful. In the words of any eager first-year law student, "There is offer, acceptance, and consideration." Yet, there are reasons why such "free consent" deserves further scrutiny. A woman's participation in surrogacy and egg-donor programs most often includes a financial reward. Helena Ragoné discovered that the family income of married surrogates averaged $38,700 and unmarried surrogates earned between $16,000 and $24,000. Since surrogates are paid a minimum fee of $8,000, it would seem that "a woman's economic status helps construct her 'will' to sell her womb."[69]

> Dr. Howard Adelman, a psychologist who screens breeder candidates for Surrogate Mother Ltd., . . . told *Ob/Gyn News*: "I believe candidates with an element of financial need are the safest. If a woman is on unemployment and has children to care for, she is not likely to change her mind and want to keep the baby she is being paid to have for someone else."[70]

These "employment opportunity" advertisements often appear in college newspapers. For example, *Washington Square News* (New York University's student-run newspaper) ran an ad the entire spring of 1997 from a "loving couple" who promised a generous sum to a "young, healthy woman." The promise of ten thousand dollars may be tempting to a young woman with large financial loans and debt who is unable to obtain a similarly lucrative job while remaining in school full-time.

Economic incentives aside, social worker Margaret Adams recognizes that advertisements and literature asking for women to "give

90

the gift of life" create a "compassion trap."[71] In an article that laments the moral celebration of women's altruism, Janice Raymond also cites this application of emotional pressure upon women. She claims that surrogate programs prey upon women's perceived role as nurturer and provider, specifically noting the work of one surrogate broker: "Noel Keane . . . has made an educational video called 'A Special Lady' which is often shown to teenage girls in high schools and other contexts, encouraging them to consider 'careers' as surrogates."[72] We have all seen the talk show episodes and grocery-store-counter magazine articles about the "generous" woman who serves as surrogate for her daughter and son-in-law or the "devoted" twin sister. This story is billed as one of courage and love. Such appreciation for the altruistic woman creates a climate of pressure and expectation with which individual women must contend. Is the fertile woman selfish for not wanting to lend her womb? Because of economic and social pressures, it is dubious at best to accept a woman's decision to be the means of fulfilling another's right to procreative liberty as an act of truly free consent.

To summarize, constitutional privacy has meant that some women have gained greater access to reproductive technology while poor, minority, young, lesbian, unmarried, and geographically disadvantaged women have not. If racial, class, age, and geographic distinctions are ignored and possibly exaggerated, large proportions of women remain excluded from the benefits that state neutrality appears to promise. Further, by fostering universal procreative liberty, women may be reduced to catalysts for others' expression of freedom. Policies that promote individual self-determination cannot be labeled advocacy of "women's liberation" if, at best, only some women benefit. Rosalind Pollack Petchesky argues that the constitutional privacy approach to alleviating the oppression of women "tends to be isolated rather than part of a total revolutionary program."[73]

Why is "pro-choice" and other privacy terminology so widely used by feminists? First, feminists embrace the right to privacy because it is efficacious. It is important to remember that feminists did not craft the constitutional right to privacy. The Supreme Court did. However, the lawyers and activists who wanted to make reproductive technology legal promoted state neutrality, choice, and procreation because these goods were palatable for both the public and the courts. Suzanne Staggenbourg's sociological dissection of the organization of the pro-choice movement concludes that professional leadership, formalized organizational structures, and certain terminology were adopted not solely on the basis of principle, but also efficacy.[74] Public-opinion polls led activists to use "pro-choice" slogans rather than "birth control" or "abortion rights" epithets because the term "choice" had wider public appeal. The name "Planned Parenthood" was adopted to replace Margaret Sanger's more controversial "American Birth Control League," despite her protests.[75] Also, Marian Faux's *Crusaders: Voices from the Abortion Front* shows how some pioneers of the "pro-choice" movement, including attorney Frank Susman and president of Catholics for a Free Choice Frances Kissling, tempered their methods and arguments for popular acceptance.[76] A degree of pragmatism underlay their advocacy of privacy. Thus, although privacy discourse has proved somewhat limited, feminists continue to rely upon it because they believe that some measure of success is better than none.

Second, feminists believe that the Supreme Court takes too limited a view of privacy. Kolbert argues that state neutrality should dictate that the state make all reproductive technology feasible to all people under the neutrality principle. Rachel Pine and Sylvia Law suggest that the Supreme Court could and should adopt a concept of reproductive freedom that would obligate the government to ensure "affirmative liberty."[77] In other words, the idea of privacy is not flawed in itself; rather, the Supreme Court has been mistaken in its narrow application and vision of it as state abstention. However, the following pages argue that privacy itself is not necessarily a powerful feminist framework.

The Feminist Privacy Framework

The two main reasons that feminists such as Lori Andrews, Wendy McElroy, Carmel Shalev, Marjorie Shultz, and Judith Jarvis Thompson advocate the concept of privacy are (1) endorsement of choice as a means of self-determination and (2) reverence for the liberating potential of capitalism.

Used to promote everything from Pepsi ("the choice of a new

generation") to peanut butter ("choosy moms choose Jif"), "choice" is a highly prized value in American society. Although it became popular as a friendly synonym for abortion rights, choice has been inflated to include other reproductive arrangements and technologies under the name "reproductive choice." According to Janice Raymond, a strong critic of privacy feminists:

> Over the last five years especially, many pro-choice advocates have emphasized that people of conscience must support new reproductive arrangements such as embryo freezing, IVF, and surrogacy, arguing for expanded access to these procedures not only for infertile women and men, but also for single and lesbian women, single and homosexual men, and various minority and economically disadvantaged groups.[78]

The old adage, "More is better than less," has been adopted by some pro-choice feminists. Fifty years ago, an infertile woman had the options of adoption or prayer, but today she also has the legal options of embryo freezing and transfer, surrogacy, or IVF. Women are purported to be better off because a plethora of infertility treatments exist today where once there were few options. Although the success rates for many infertility treatments are still very low while the costs remain high, the fact that women numerically have more options today than yesterday is celebrated. These options are revered because respect for a woman's right to form and pursue her own preferences as a rational and capable individual promotes her self-determination. The decision regarding what device to employ among a field of possibilities is valued, since it is assumed that the probability for satisfying desires is improved, fostering greater autonomy.

Positive notions of choice ground capitalistic visions of market consumption, as the spending power of individual agents is valued over the impact on society and the individual consumer, and moral implications of the good in question are ignored. Friedrich von Hayek outlined the basic virtues of the free-market system in *The Mirage of Social Justice.* This famous critique of indemnification regards government distribution and market regulation as the loss of individual freedom, since choice and free will are limited. Fearing the oppressive arm of the state, Hayek notes that whenever individual liberty is violated, the government approaches nearer and nearer to a totalitarian system.[79] Many pro-choice feminists favor extending these laissez-faire notions to women, specifically the right to purchase IVF, surrogacy, anesthesia, and abortion.[80] They accept the capitalist system as an embodiment of freedom from state oppression and therefore demand inclusion in the free market, believing that philosophies of maximized consumer choice best respect the self-determination of individuals. Therefore, in addition to cherishing a mass quantity of options as necessarily enhancing consumer freedom, Wendy McElroy and some other privacy feminists relish the right to choose because it represents the absence of state constraint. According to libertarian philosopher Robert Nozick, "The minimal state is the most extensive state that can be justified. Any state more extensive violates people's rights."[81]

Thus far, the explanations of choice and capitalism as precious feminist goods (in other words, things which foster self-determination) have focused upon the consumer aspects of reproductive technology. In an article in *Differences: A Journal of Feminist Cultural Studies*, Alys Eve Weinbaum argued that feminists should comprehend reproductive labor as socially valuable, "reclaiming the material body as the appropriable means of production."[82] Weinbaum reasons for recognition of the individual (woman) as potential laborer. Replacing the model of "women are mothers" with "women are laborers" is anti-essentialist. She stresses the nature of reproduction as production. By viewing women as potential participants in the market economy, Weinbaum reconstructs pregnancy as an individual activity or skill.

> A Marxist understanding of reproduction as productive with a feminist discussion of the possibilities for renarrativizing the materiality of the maternal body . . . a reformulation of reproduction as (re)production [dictates] the conceptual collapse of the binarism of production/reproduction, reproduction as a gendered activity ceases to exist.[83]

Consequently, Weinbaum implicitly argues for women's inclusion in the free-market system as producers, recognizing the feminist potential of capitalism. Carmel Shalev uses a similarly labor-sensitive analysis of reproduction in her book about surrogacy: "My argument is that a concept of wages for reproduction can transform reproductive consciousness in a manner that transcends male-female biological difference to an androgynous mode of human being, while allowing women to reclaim the procreative power that has been subsumed under patriarchy as a mark of their inferiority."[84]

Finally, these feminists believe that it is the ultimate expression of freedom to make an agreement reinforcing or acting upon personal preference. The ability to contract is hailed as the act of self-determination. These feminists (and perhaps Nozick) promote respect for women's free consent to technological intervention in the womb as reverence for women as rational individuals, that is, as equal citizens. As mentioned in the discussion of constitutional privacy, Shalev applauds the appropriation of contract law to "reproductive collaboration" (arrangements like surrogacy and egg donation). Free from government regulation, the general rules of contract law—the meeting of the minds regarding an exchange of binding promises—are applicable.[85] Like any other free compact, these agreements are sacred, and third-party objections are deemed impotent: "The right to make mistakes and to select the wrong choice might be seen as the cornerstone of liberal thought. The individual is sovereign and should not be constrained simply on the grounds of another's disapproval."[86] The consequences of these decisions are not valued as much as the ability to decide a course of action freely. The termination of an unintended pregnancy and the sweet sleep of anesthetics during childbirth are not championed in themselves as much as the ability to choose these options free from government restraint. In contrast to technophilia, perhaps the privacy approach is techno-neutral. In fact, some privacy advocates who value a woman's right to choose abortion or surrogacy claim not to believe personally in the practice.[87] It is the principle of free choice that is prized, not technology itself.

Critique of the Feminist Privacy Perspective

I argue that privacy feminists are misguided in their acceptance, indeed promulgation, of choice and consumerism as goods that necessarily contribute to women's liberation from oppression by fomenting self-determination.

Unbridled free choice is not necessarily woman-friendly.

The classic feminist critique of systems that depend upon free consent argues that women are incapable of free choice for two reasons.

First, women are "coerced" by their partners and social pressure to enter contracts regarding IVF or abortion. Catharine MacKinnon argues that the division of society into two sexes underlies all social relations, and it is women's experience of sexual objectification that is the true core of our oppression. Although some women may claim to be free from such constraints and able to make contracts from equal standing with clear conscience (she specifically refers to a woman's supposedly free decision to pose for pornographic footage), these women are merely suffering from false consciousness:

> Women's acceptance of their condition does not contradict its fundamental unacceptability if women have little choice but to become persons who freely choose women's roles. For this reason, the reality of women's oppression is, finally, neither demonstrative nor refutable empirically.[88]

Choice is illusory in a culture that defines a woman's identity in terms of motherhood because a woman cannot remove herself and her decisions from this social context and forced identification. When society brands the childless woman "barren," like a flawed, useless plot of land, can her decision to undergo IVF treatment truly constitute an act of individual will? "The right to choose ignores the feminist truth that in a male supremacist society, no choice a woman makes is entirely free or in her interest."[89] Any decision to use IVF, surrogacy, abortion, and so on must be recognized as a social decision rather than isolated, pure individual preferences. Decision making cannot be said to be an act of self-determination if women's "self" is socially constructed and independently unidentifiable. Consequently, this critique labels contractual agreement and indeed capitalism itself to be reflective of, if not reinforcing, patriarchy.

Second, feminists such as Carol Rose might be skeptical of feminist celebration of free choice because the methods themselves—bartering and contracting—involve attributes culturally marked as masculine. Arguing that women have a "taste for cooperation" that helps account for the unequal distribution of assets in society between women and men, Rose might be wary of women's ability to fairly contract out our wombs or sell our eggs from an equal bargaining position.[90]

Even if a woman is able to identify her own will free from social pressure (contrary to MacKinnon) and she has escaped the essentialist femininity (described by Rose), contract making with a male doctor or her husband might still constitute an unequal bargaining arrangement. It is possible to adhere to a more liberal social-constructionist view and still recognize the danger of feminists embracing bartering and contracting because constructions (such as unequal education, work wages, and so on) negate the possibility of equal bargaining positions.[91]

Although these arguments about the implications of choice and contract theory are provocative, they leave women with little redress short of revolution. Moreover, these criticisms apply to women's ability to contract more generally. Might we be able to fairly select a pair of shoes or a loaf of bread and barter a price with the man selling them to us? There are better reasons why women should be skeptical about "free choice."

In an article by the same title, Gerald Dworkin asked, "Is more choice better than less?"[92] He argued that the *quantity* of alternatives does not necessarily improve the *quality* of alternatives. Although agreeing with privacy feminists who believe self-determination to be a crucial facet (if not *the* crucial facet) of the good life, Dworkin explains that, for the rational individual, more choices are not always preferable to fewer:

> What has intrinsic value is not having choices but being recognized as the kind of creature who is capable of making choices . . . and a moral agent equally worthy of respect by all. . . . This would at most support the view that, with respect to a certain range of choices, it is desirable to have *some* options.[93]

Accordingly, feminists should not blindly celebrate the mere number of legal contraceptives without regard for the specific impact these options have on women's bodies and lives. Imagine FDA approval of a 100 percent effective contraceptive drink—that comes in an array of delicious, fat-free flavors. Should we celebrate this miracle liquid if it also causes heart palpitations and seizures, is forced upon low-income women as a condition for welfare benefits and child custody, and its reversal involves great expense and a long waiting list? Should we blindly defend all FDA-approved contraceptives? The health and safety implications of these devices should be examined and their value determined with regard for their side effects, risks, costs, social implications, and so on. Only after the value of a new device (or potable) has been assessed should feminists rejoice in proportion to its worth, rather than in honor of the mere existence of another choice.

Moreover, technological intervention in the womb is often driven by racially charged impetus. With respect to infertility treatments, procreative liberty is another way of saying, "I want a baby that is genetically like me," a sentiment that is often racially charged. Dorothy Roberts argues that "the legitimacy of these technologies depends upon the production of white children," lamenting both the commodification of women and the devaluation of black reproduction.[94] Privacy feminists erroneously solemnize the principle of individual choice at the expense of failing to recognize the array of effects from the various devices, instead believing that the means justify the ends.

Capitalism is not necessarily woman-friendly.

While liberal feminists such as Zillah Eisenstein claim that the link between capitalism and patriarchy can be broken with the entry of women in massive numbers into the workforce,[95] others are less optimistic about feminist influence on capitalism. Indeed, Juliet Mitchell and bell hooks have each labeled the tendency within the women's movement to cooperate with capitalism "bourgeois feminism."[96]

Competitive market systems are more concerned with profit than feminism. Devices are made with supply and demand in mind, and women's comfort, practicality, and so on are considered only to the extent that demand is affected. Simply, market-enhanced options are not necessarily better options because market systems of supply and demand do not necessarily value safety or reliability.

Also, the marketing of women's parts and functions through surrogacy or embryo transfer, for example, serves to turn sections of a woman's body into objects worthy of financial reward:

> If commodification simply means that the material in question has been made a commodity, and exchanged for valuable consideration, it is simply another term to describe the transaction. . . . However, critics frequently use the term to include negative consequences, especially those that result in objectification . . . ways of thinking about organs, attitudes, sentiments, etc. . . . Terms of debasement and degradation play a role.[97]

Weinbaum believes that the identification of the body as a material resource is simple fact, if not feminist compliment. Moreover, how is women's reproductive work different from other forms of manual labor, such as professional sports, construction work, or housekeeping? These questions and arguments ignore the historical degradation of women's work, contributions, activities, and so on. Contracts occur in the context of a given situation and power structure. Heidi Hartman recognizes the constant interdependency of capitalism and patriarchy:

> Capitalism grew on top of patriarchy; patriarchal capitalism is stratified society par excellence. . . . If women are to be free, they must fight against both patriarchal power and capitalist organization of society. . . . Because the sexual division of labor and male domination are so long-standing, it will be very difficult to eradicate them and impossible to eradicate the former without the latter.[98]

She argues that competitive market systems necessarily lead to hierarchical structures; since sexual division of labor consistently deems women's work as unskilled and unpaid, women are devalued. Consequently, capitalism must be recognized as inherently patriarchal.

Also, women are severed from their selves through commodification. As individual parts and services of the body are deemed valuable in their own right, the oppositional relationship between a woman and her body (the adversarial approach to pregnancy) is enhanced. When eggs, the fetus, or the functions of the womb possess independent value, medical and state intervention is inspired.

If the job of a surrogate is to produce a healthy baby, then the survival of the fetus she carries is of great economic significance. The fetus is recognized as possessing its own financial value like any other good or service. A surrogate may be asked to refrain from smoking, drinking, driving a car, or sitting in front of a video display terminal because an infertile couple's investment is in her care. These commodities become of increasing importance, and the woman necessarily loses control of her whole self.

The disembodiment caused by contractual notions of human reproduction was highlighted by Patricia Williams in her reflections following Judge Sorkow's decision in the Baby M case. In addition to noting the racial overtones of "buying a baby just like me," she wrote about Whitehead's powerlessness in the face of the contract she signed and the inadequacy of contract law to respond to the realities of our complicated, dynamic lives:

> Contract law reduces life to fairy tale. The four corners of the agreement become parent. Performance is the equivalent of obedience to the parent. Obedience is dutifully passive. Passivity is valued as good contract-socialized behavior; activity is caged in retrospective hypotheses about states of mind at the magic moment of contracting. Nonperformance is disobedience; disobedience is active; activity becomes evil in contrast to the childlike passivity of contract conformity.[99]

Consequently, privacy feminists should reconsider their celebration of capitalist approaches to reproductive technology, since promoting legal and available technology in the name of a right to consumption may in fact serve to deflate women's self-determination and alienate us from our own bodies.

Privacy is not necessarily a feminist ideal.

Reflecting back to *Webster's* definition of privacy as "seclusion" and considering the nature of privacy itself, feminists would be wise to reconsider their acceptance of this concept. Patriarchy has always depended upon a dichotomy between the public and private realm, the latter largely associated with women, the family, and unpaid, unglamorous work. "The classical citizen of Athens knew that there was a difference between the public and private—and resolved any possibility of a paradox by disavowing the worth of private life. The public life was the only recognized life."[100] From Greece to Rome to Rousseau to Locke, the family, marriage and women have been acknowledged as occupying a separate—and less glorious, to say the least—sphere.[101] When what happens in the private realm is considered to be of less political importance than what happens in the public realm, and decisions concerning reproduction are deemed acts of "privacy," such acts are given a negative connotation.

Moreover, the private realm has historically been associated with legal subordination of women—from legal marital rape and abuse to married women's property laws. Rhonda Copelon condemned reverence for the public/private dichotomy on the basis of this ugly record:

> It is compatible with a legal tradition of non-interference in marriage; a tradition that denied women legal relief from economic and physical abuse by their husbands; a tradition that had long served to reinforce male dominance in the home. Privacy buttresses the conservative idea that the personal is separate from the political, and that the larger social structure has no impact on private, individual choice. The privacy framework assumes that society bears no affirmative responsibility for individual choice or action.[102]

The critiques of privacy mentioned so far condemn what Cass Sunstein and Anita Allen have each called "conventional privacy;" the definition of privacy as "seclusion" or "isolation," the notion of a separate space, typically of lower political status and occupied by women. However, so-called "decisional privacy" is also an unpromising hero.

There are negative consequences when centuries-old procedures and devices such as abortion, surrogacy, and therapeutic insemination are shrouded as "private choices." Thus, contraception, assisted conception, and birthing techniques as conscious activities are labeled "unnatural." Rather than recognize these devices and techniques as daily realities of women's health (like food, clothing, and shelter), these activities are viewed as "frivolous acts," or "life's extras," stigmatizing women and fostering guilt. Joan Williams sug-

101

gests that pro-choice rhetoric "awakens gender fears about selfish mothers destroying babies to pursue their own self-interest."[103] Abortion is viewed as a narcissistic decision rather than a routine "rite" of life and infertility treatment is viewed as an outlandish act of desperation. These activities are labeled selfish, inspiring negative social and psychological connotations rather than cultivating acceptance as responsible and justifiable realities of women's lives.

Furthermore, rather than exalting fertility control or the enhanced ability to conceive or the use of anesthetics during pregnancy, women whisper about their experiences, if silence is broken at all. Abortions and failed infertility treatments remain secrets. The assigned "private" nature of these common occurrences truncates the possibility of open discussion. By not sharing these experiences with each other, women are unable to recognize these acts and decisions as a common female sagacity. The possibility of a "collective conscience" is eliminated, as women remain atomistic and alienated from each other. Feminists such as Sheila Rowbotham and Catharine MacKinnon define this "collective conscience" differently, but both view this awareness as a necessary condition for women's liberation; consciousness-raising is politically significant.[104]

Rowbotham argues that through discussion and exchange with others, women come to recognize their own oppression. Although all women are subjected and must recognize their subjection through interaction, this identification is an independent epiphany:

> In order to create an alternative an oppressed group must at once shatter the self-reflecting world which encircles it and, at the same time, project its own image onto history. In order to discover its own identity as distinct from that of the oppressor it has to become visible to itself. All revolutionary movements create their own ways of seeing. But this is a result of great labor. . . . The first step is to connect and learn and trust one another.[105]

MacKinnon's understanding of this feminist awareness is more united in nature, as exchanges between women lead to a collective recognition and rebellion—much like the class revolution described by Marx.[106] Indeed, speak-outs organized by feminists in the 1970s (like the Redstockings in New York City) were designed to give women the opportunity to talk about their personal experiences and motivate mass action.

Regardless of their differences, both Rowbotham and MacKinnon think that the suppression of this epiphany and the collective experience of oppression are fostered by the private/public dichotomy. MacKinnon and Rowbotham both argue for the need of women to associate and grow in congruence with other women, while the pro-choice feminist's advocacy of privacy does not necessarily respect the universal nature of women's oppression and the liberating potential of exchange. This condemnation not only chides the promotion of privacy, but also feminist reverence for individualism.

Individualism does not necessarily promote the well-being of women.

Perhaps the most noted feminist defense of reproductive self-determination is Judith Jarvis Thompson's parable about waking up in bed to find yourself physically connected to an unconscious famous violinist. He is physically dependent upon you for life support.[107] (Your kidneys extract poisons from his blood as well as your own.) What are your responsibilities to this unwanted freeloader? Despite having made the dependent agent a human being (indeed, a *famous* violinist) and creating a clear life-or-death situation, Thompson determines that you owe no duty to the dependent. Consistent with moral determinations about the injustice of trespassing, forced servitude, and the lack of duty to rescue, the person attached to the famous violinist as well as the woman with the unwanted pregnancy deserve autonomy. Consequently, abortion is morally justified.

Like Thompson, advocates of the right to technological intervention in the womb in the name of privacy are concerned with fostering the self-determination of all individuals and not necessarily the well-being of women. If the Firestone-Haraway perspective hoped to establish equality of result, Alison Jaggar describes the privacy feminist view as championing "the equal opportunity of each individual, regardless of sex, to seek whatever social position she or he wishes. Freedom is primarily the absence of legal constraints to hinder women in this enterprise."[108] Consequently, androcentric language is utilized; for example, Purdy refers to unwanted pregnancy "drafting" women into motherhood[109] and Thompson's hypothetical characters are mostly male, tangled in gender-free, nonsexual situations such as trespassing and sharing a box of chocolates. Thus, these feminists apply the universal theory of civil liberties to women, believing that all individuals, by the fact of their existence, are guaranteed a certain set of rights. Privacy advocates ask that women be "treated as individuals, rather than as potential mothers."[110] In other words, privacy feminists define equal treatment as the same treatment. Zillah Eisenstein explains this brand of feminism as the promise of liberalism extended to women.[111] This vision of the good life involves uninfringed self-determination for all individuals, and women are, above all, individuals.

If the common aspects among all individuals are stressed, how are the unique interests and needs of women compensated? Does ignoring gender—the social position of females in society—as a significant fact of being minimize the effects of gender? (If you close your eyes, will it truly disappear?)

Although these feminists can point to the real legal gains they have made, others deplore the fact that this group of feminists have created policies that serve the good of a few white, middle to upperclass women and ignore, if not sacrifice, the reproductive freedom of all women and the reality of gender more generally.

Because of the existing power relations, advocating unrestrained capitalism and privacy in the name of individualism cannot be assumed to benefit women. If the choices and decisions women make are expressions of individual liberty, can sexual equality be said to be promoted? Or has the liberty of individuals been promoted, regardless of sex? As Joan Williams notes:

> What we need, then, is a rule that avoids the traditional correlation between gender and sex, a rule that is sex, but not gender, neutral. . . . The core feminist goal is not one of pretending gender does not exist. Instead, it is to deinstitutionalize the gendered structure of our society.[112]

Conclusion

Although there are many problems with both constitutional privacy and a feminist notion of privacy, we should understand them and extract the most positive elements of these theories. Certainly bodily autonomy should be an important element of any feminist response to technological intervention in the womb that respects the diversity of women because we should be able to determine our own reproductive destiny according to our particular needs and preferences. Moreover, the experience of constitutional privacy informs our understanding of judicial, social, and political efficacy: an appeal to individual freedom may be expedient.

Notes

1. "Feminists have traditionally made their political demands in terms of rights." Elizabeth Kingdom, *What's Wrong with Rights?* (Edinburgh: Edinburgh University Press, 1991), 4. Consider the right to vote, the right to access to education, the right to enlist in the military, and so on as enumerated or unenumerated subpleas for self-determination. Moreover, Jennifer Nedelsky argues that at the core of American rights discourse is the protection of private property, a vestige of the founders' preoccupation with land. Jennifer Nedelsky, *Private Property and the Limits of American Constitutionalism: The Madisonian Framework and Its Legacy* (Chicago: University of Chicago Press, 1990).

2. Ruth Bader Ginsburg, testimony before the Senate Judiciary Committee Report published 5 August 1993, 103d Cong., 1st sess., *Exec. Report* 103–06, 13.

3. For a discussion of constitutional interpretation, see David Richards, *Foundations of American Constitutionalism* (New York: Oxford University Press, 1989).

4. Webster, 677.

5. David Garrow, *Liberty and Sexuality* (New York: Macmillan, 1994), 260. This book narrates the complete history of the right to privacy as it applies to sexuality. It is extraordinarily thorough.

6. Warren, Earl, and Louis Brandeis, "The Right to Privacy," *Harvard Law Review* (1890): 193–220. One hundred years later, an impressive list of law review articles speculates on the legacy of this famous article. See Garrow, 783, fn. 83.

7. *Griswold v. Connecticut*, 381 U.S. 479 (1965).

8. For example, see *Eisenstadt v. Baird*, 405 U.S. 438 (1972).

9. *Roe v. Wade*, 410 U.S. 113 (1973) (striking down Texas statute criminalizing abortion); *Doe v. Bolton*, 410 U.S. 179 (1973) (Georgia companion case).

10. 410 U.S. at 159.

11. *Planned Parenthood v. Casey*, 112 S. Ct. 2791, 2817–18 (1992).

12. 112 S. Ct. at 2797.

13. 112 S. Ct. at 2818 ("We reject the trimester framework, which we do not consider to be part of the essential holding of *Roe*.").

14. 112 S. Ct. at 2798.

15. 112 S. Ct. at 2811.

16. 112 S. Ct. at 2799.

17. 112 S. Ct. at 2825.

18. See Janet Benshoof, "Abortion Rights and Wrongs: Undue Burdens—The Rhetoric is Pro-Roe, but the Reality is Anti-Choice," *The Nation* (14 October 1996): 19–20.

19. Dawn Johnsen, "Shared Interests: Promoting Healthy Births without Sacrificing Women's Liberty," *Hastings Law Journal* 43 (1992): 569–614, 571 (arguing that the strict scrutiny standard of review suggests that the adversarial approach to pregnancy be forsaken, replaced with a facilitative approach).

20. 410 U.S. at 162.

21. Ruth Colker, *Abortion & Dialogue* (Bloomington: Indiana University Press, 1992), 146.

22. Colker, 154.

23. Veronica E. B. Kolder et al., "Court-Ordered Obstetrical Interventions," *New England Journal of Medicine* (1987): 1192–. Also see the work of Janet Gallagher listed in the bibliography. Also see *Jefferson v. Griffin Spalding County Hospital Authority*, 274 S.E.2d 457 (Ga. 1981) (citing Roe to support its determination, the Supreme Court of Georgia held that because a viable fetus has a right to state protection against abortion, this right must also include the right of the viable fetus to potentially lifesaving treatment).

24. *People v. Stewart*, No. M508197 (Cal. Mun. Ct. Feb. 26, 1987); *In re Steven S.*, 126 Cal. App. 3d 23 (1981), "To Stop Abortion by Addict, Her Brother Steps In," *New York Times*, 23 February 1992, 24); *Grodin v. Grodin*, 301 N.W.2d 869 (Mich. Ct. App. 1980); *In re Jeffrey*, No. 99851 (Mich. Ct. App. Apr. 9, 1987).

25. See ACLU memoranda, 15 February 1990, "Discriminatory Punishment of Pregnant Women" and 7 February 1990, "Case Update." Excerpts from these memoranda are reprinted in *From Abortion to Reproductive Freedom*, Marlene Gerber Fried, ed. (Boston: South End Press, 1990), 269–70.

26. Reported in *Reproductive Freedom News*, The Center For Reproductive Law and Policy, New York (4 October 1996).

27. Alida Brill, *Nobody's Business: The Paradoxes of Privacy* (Reading, Mass.: Addison-Wesley, 1990), 85. State-imposed nonconsensual invasions of the womb are especially noxious when one considers the fact that, in *Winston v. Lee*, the Supreme Court held that intrusive surgery can not be imposed upon a criminal suspect to dislodge a bullet (evidence of criminal involvement) from the suspect's chest. 410 U.S. 753 (1985). For an earlier discussion of court-ordered Cesareans in the context of court-ordered surgery more generally, see Nancy Rhoden, "The Judge in the Delivery Room: The Emergence of Court-Ordered Cesarean Sections," *California Law Review* (1986): 1951–2030. Also see the work of Janet Gallagher listed in the bibliography.

28. Henry M. Sondheimer, "The Fetus is the Only Patient," *The Hastings Center Report* (August 1983): 50. True, women may desire attention and care for their fetuses; however, the identification of fetal viability has encouraged many doctors to provide such services regardless of the woman's sentiment. See *In re Jamaica Hospital*, 491 N.Y.S.2d 898 (N.Y. Sup. Ct. 1985) (ordering a blood transfusion to protect the life of a midterm fetus over objections of the mother). Lawyer Lynn Paltrow, formerly of the Center for Reproductive Law and Policy and now with Planned Parenthood of New York City, was counsel for many of these cases and is largely responsible for the increasing recognition of these court orders as serious threats to women's bodily autonomy and political equality. Similarly, see the work of barrister Barbara Hewson in Great Britain.

29. For an in-depth discussion of state-by-state abortion politics, consult Malcolm L. Goggin, ed. *Understanding the New Politics of Abortion* (London: Sage, 1993). Also, contact NARAL in Washington, D.C., for up-to-minute monitoring of abortion legislation nationwide. NARAL reports that in 1995, 171 anti-choice bills were introduced, compared with 97 in 1994, a 76 percent increase. Also in 1995, anti-choice legislation was introduced in forty-four states, compared with thirty in 1994, a 47 percent increase. See NARAL, *Who Decides? A State-by-State Review of Abortion and Reproductive Rights* (Washington, D.C.).

30. Rhonda Copelon, "From Privacy to Autonomy: The Conditions for Sexual and Reproductive Freedom," in *From Abortion to Reproductive Freedom: Transforming a Movement*, Marlene Gerber Fried, ed. (Boston: South End Press, 1990), 36.

31. Katherine De Gama, "A Brave New World?" in *Feminist Theory and Legal Strategy*, Anne Bottomley and Joanne Conaghan, eds. (Oxford: Blackwell, 1992), 118.

32. Recently, there have been some interesting developments regarding forced technological intervention in the womb which may signal a new trend. In Washington, D.C., a pregnant Angela Carder was diagnosed with terminal bone cancer and was denied chemotherapy by her doctors because of its potential effects on the fetus. However, in *In re A.C.*, the Court held "in virtually all cases the decision of the patient . . . will control. We do not quite foreclose the possibility that a conflicting state interest may be so compelling that the patient's wishes must yield, but we anticipate that such cases will be extremely rare and truly exceptional." 573 A.2d 1235, 1252 (D.C. 1990). Also, a young married Chicago woman ("Mother Doe") who was thirty-five weeks pregnant with her first child refused to submit to a Cesarean section to alleviate a medical condition that delivered insufficient oxygen to the fetus such that a doctor testified in court that the fetus would have close to a 0 percent chance of surviving natural birth. The state's request for temporary custody (of the fetus) was denied and the court, citing *In re A.C.*, held that "a woman's competent choice in refusing a medical treatment as invasive as a Cesarean section during her pregnancy must be honored, even in circumstances where the choice may be harmful to her fetus." *Baby Boy Doe v. Mother Doe*, 632 N.E.2d 326 (Ill. App.),

cert. denied, 114 S. Ct. 652 (1994) (court found that the right of a competent pregnant woman to refuse medical treatment arose from her rights to privacy, bodily integrity, and religious liberty). The complexity and unevenness in this area of the law serve to substantiate my argument for a comprehensive response to technological intervention in the womb.

33. On the need to redefine the relationship between science and law, see Nancy Rhoden, "Trimesters and Technology: Revamping Roe v. Wade," *Yale Law Journal* (1986): 639–97.

34. De Gama, 119.

35. The Center for Reproductive Law and Policy (CRLP), 120 Wall Street, New York, New York, has been an extremely productive and effective legal advocate for reproductive choice since its founding in June 1992. Indeed, their legal approach to technological intervention in the womb is holistic, as they argue cases and submit briefs not only on various technologies and arrangements, but also in a plethora of international settings.

36. "Amicus Brief for *Webster vs. Reproductive Services* on Behalf of Seventy-Five Women's Organizations," *Women's Rights Law Reporter* (Fall/Winter 1989): 256.

37. *Maher v. Roe*, 432 U.S. 464 (1977) (no requirement for state to fund terminations for impoverished women, nor does regulation impinge upon fundamental right to privacy); *Harris v. McRae*, 448 U.S. 297 (1980) (Hyde amendment prohibiting federal reimbursement for termination deemed constitutional); *Webster v. Reproductive Health Services*, 492 U.S. 490 (1990) (upholding statute allowing *inter alia* for prohibition on use of public employees or facilities to perform terminations).

38. Kolbert, 1164.

39. As discussed in Athena Liu, *Artificial Reproduction and Reproductive Rights* (Hong Kong: Dartmouth Publishing, 1991).

40. *Skinner v. Oklahoma*, 316 U.S. 535, 536 (1942).

41. 316 U.S. at 541.

42. Liu, 32.

43. John Robertson, *Children of Choice: Freedom and the New Reproductive Technologies* (Princeton: Princeton University Press, 1994), 4. For an interesting literature review, see Joan C. Callahan, "Procreative Liberty: Whose Procreation, Whose Liberty?" *Stanford Law and Policy Review* (1995): 121–25.

44. Janice Raymond, *Women as Wombs* (New York: Harper Collins, 1993), 77.

45. For some of the strongest pro-surrogacy statements made by a feminist, see the work of Lori Andrews listed in the bibliography.

46. Although he did negate the clause that purported to take control of Whitehead's right to abortion as against public policy. *In re Baby M*, 525 A.2d 1128, 1159 (N.J. 1987) (Judge Sorkow).

47. 525 A.2d at 1164.

48. *In the Matter of Baby M*, 537 A.2d 1227 (N.J. 1988) (Judge Wilentz invalidating

the surrogacy contract because it conflicted with the law and public policy of New Jersey, but awarding custody to the biological father).

49. *Johnson v. Calvert*, 851 P.2d 776, 776 (1993). See also Eric Horstmeyer, "Gestational Surrogacy," *University of Louisville Journal of Family Law* 32 (1994): 953–59; Martin Kasindorf, "And Baby Makes Four," *Los Angeles Times Magazine* 20 January 1991: 10–16, 30–33.

50. Marjorie Shultz, "Reproductive Technology and Intent-Based Parenthood: An Opportunity for Gender Neutrality," *Wisconsin Law Review* (1990): 290–398. She argues that feminists should embrace the new reproductive opportunities as enhancing the potential for expression and effectuation of personal intentions.

51. 851 P.2d at 781.

52. Marlene Gerber Fried and Loretta Ross, "Reproductive Freedom: Our Right to Decide," *Open Pamphlet Series* (Westfield, N.J.: Open Media, 1992): 9.

53. Frances Olsen, "Unraveling Compromise," *Harvard Law Review* (1989): 105–135, 113 ("the abortion funding cases highlight . . . limitations of the privacy analysis"); Deborah Rhode, "Reproductive Freedom," in *Feminist Jurisprudence*, Patricia Smith, ed. (New York: Oxford University Press, 1993), 305–21, 311 ("The focus on privacy also has helped rationalize the Supreme Court's subsequent decisions upholding withdrawal of public funds for abortion services."). See also note 37.

54. NARAL, *Who Decides? A State by State Review of Abortion Rights*, 4th ed. (Washington: NARAL Foundation, 1993).

55. Peter J. Neumann, et al., "The Cost of Successful Delivery with In Vitro Fertilization," *New England Journal of Medicine* 331 (1994): 239–43. Also, Marnie Mueller, "Financing High-Tech Reproductive Medical Expenditures," *Stanford Law and Policy Review* (1995): 113–118.

56. Helena Ragoné reports that the average income of women who seek infertility treatment is over $35,000 per year, and the average husband's income is over $58,000 per year. Furthermore, every husband in the cases she considered had at least a university degree, with most having completed graduate work. Helena Ragoné, *Surrogate Motherhood* (Oxford: Westview Press, 1994), 90. Consequently, surrogacy arrangements do not seem any more equitable than the biblical days of Sarah and Hagar the slave-girl.

57. *Bellotti v. Baird*, 443 U.S. 622 (1979); *Akron v. Akron Center for Reproductive Health*, 462 U.S. 416 (1983); *Webster v. Reproductive Health Services*, 492 U.S. 490 (1990); *Planned Parenthood v. Casey*, 112 S. Ct. 2791 (1992).

58. Under *Bellotti*, states that require parental consent must provide a (sometimes judicial) bypass clause whereby minors (under eighteen years old) can seek the permission of a judge rather than that of a parent who might be hostile, involved with the pregnancy, or detained. See Appendix B for a complete list of state by state minors' access to abortion. Although *Carey v. Population Planning Services*, 410 U.S. 678 (1977) held that it is unconstitutional to require teens to notify their

109

parents before procuring over-the-counter contraception, NARAL reports that squeal rules have been applied to other forms of contraception.

59. Brill, 20.

60. Angela Bonavoglia, "Kathy's Day in Court," in *From Abortion to Reproductive Freedom: Transforming a Movement*, Marlene Gerber Fried, ed. (Boston: South End Press, 1990). This article provides a description of the dangerous (many would say "undue") burden these squeal rules place on young women.

61. Susan Faludi, *Backlash* (New York: Crown Publishers, 1991).

62. Becky's parents, Karen and Bill Bell, and brother, Bill Bell, Jr., are now extremely persuasive abortion-rights activists, sponsored by The Feminist Majority.

63. For an interesting discussion of the intention-based gender neutral approach to technological intervention in the womb, see Marjorie Maguire Shultz, "Reproductive Technology and Intent-Based Parenthood: An Opportunity for Gender Neutrality," *University of Wisconsin Law Review* (1990): 297–398.

64. Raymond, *Women as Wombs*, 78.

65. Raymond, 79.

66. *University Health Services v. Piazzi*, No. CV86-RCCV-464 (Super. Ct. of Richmond County, Ga., Aug. 4, 1986), as described in James Jordan, "Incubating for the State: The Precarious Autonomy of Persistently Vegetative and Brain-Dead Pregnant Women," *Georgia Law Review* (1988): 1103–65. I argue that where a woman's desires are not explicitly expressed, her natural expiration should be respected. Many states currently have laws that specify that the terminally ill or comatose patient's living will is suspended if she is pregnant. The constitutionality of such discriminatory laws, and PMV more generally, has yet to be decided. See Elizabeth Carlin Benton, "The Constitutionality of Pregnancy Clauses in Living Will Statutes," *Vanderbilt Law Review* (1990): 1821–37.

67. Ragoné even cites the example of a surrogate who resisted induced premature labor at the request of the contracting couple and the director of the program involved. Although Ragoné does explain that surrogates can request certain independent freedoms in the original contract, she also notes the lack of education and truly free consent on the part of surrogates, as well as the overbearing nature of many program directors and the high knowledge level and decisiveness of clients. Ragoné's main point is that the ability of surrogates to bargain and contract freely may be extremely impaired, especially in comparison to the other agents involved. For additional examples of the exploitation of surrogates, see Gena Corea, "Testimony before the California Assembly Judiciary Committee, April, 1988," in *Surrogate Motherhood: Politics and Privacy*, Larry Gostin, ed. (Bloomington: Indiana University Press, 1990), 325–37.

68. Jocelynne Scutt, ed., *The Baby Machine: Reproductive Technology and the Commercialisation of Motherhood* (London: Green Print, 1990).

69. Corea, 231.

70. Corea, 229.

71. As cited by Janice G. Raymond, "Reproductive Gifts and Gift Giving: The Altruistic Woman," *Hastings Center Report* (November/December 1990). Hereafter, Raymond, *Altruistic Woman.*

72. Raymond, *Altruistic Woman,* 8.

73. Rosalind Pollack Petchesky, *Abortion and Woman's Choice* (London: Verso, 1986), 7.

74. Suzanne Staggenborg, *The Pro-Choice Movement* (Oxford: Oxford University Press, 1991).

75. Ellen Chesler reported that "the name change was symbolic to Margaret of a weak and spineless leadership," *Woman of Valor: Margaret Sanger and the Birth Control Movement* (New York: Simon and Schuster, 1992), 393.

76. Marian Faux, *Crusaders: Voices from the Abortion Front* (New York: Carol Publishing, 1990).

77. Rachel Pine and Sylvia Law, "Envisioning a Future for Reproductive Liberty: Strategies for Making Rights Real," *Harvard Civil Rights-Civil Liberties Law Review* (1992): 407–63. Their feminist vision of reproductive freedom includes freedom from state control, government neutrality on matters affecting reproductive choice, and reproductive freedom as an affirmative liberty.

78. Raymond, *Women as Wombs,* 84.

79. Friedrich von Hayek, *The Mirage of Social Justice,* vol. 2 of *Law, Legislation, and Liberty* (London: Routledge, 1976).

80. For example, see the work of libertarian feminist Wendy McElroy or, *Freedom, Feminism, and State* (Washington, D.C.: Cato Institute, 1992). Also see her article in *Reason,* vol. 26 (December 1994) ("The main appeal of reproductive technologies is that they give people more choices and more flexibility in a domain previously ruled by biological chance and limits.").

81. Robert Nozick, *Anarchy, State and Utopia* (Oxford: Blackwell, 1968).

82. Alys Eve Weinbaum, "Marx, Irigaray and the Politics of Representation," *Differences: A Journal of Feminist Cultural Studies* (Providence: Brown University Press, Spring 1994), 100.

83. Weinbaum, 105.

84. Shalev, 12.

85. Shalev, 99.

86. Susan Easton, *The Problem of Pornography* (London: Routledge, 1994), 50. While it may seem strange to juxtapose a quote about pornography in the middle of a book about technological intervention in the womb, as I mentioned in the introduction, these feminist arguments can be extended to other arenas. Although focusing on a particular subject matter, my intention is to comment upon feminist practice, advocacy, and theory more generally.

87. For example, in the 1990 and 1992 elections, many politicians, including

former New York Governor Mario Cuomo, declared themselves to be "publicly pro-choice, personally anti-abortion."

88. Catharine MacKinnon, "Feminism, Marxism, Method and the State: An Agenda for Theory," in *Feminist Theory: A Critique of Ideology*, N. O. Keohane, ed. (Brighton: Harvester, 1982). Hereafter, MacKinnon, *Fem., Marx., Method.*

89. Fried and Ross, 11.

90. Carol Rose, "Women and Property: Gaining and Losing Ground," *Virginia Law Review* (1992): 209–39; "Bargaining and Gender," *Harvard Journal of Law and Public Policy* (1995): 547–63.

91. Elizabeth Frazer and Nicola Lacey remark, "We might well have hesitations about the very discourse of 'bargaining' as a legitimate device, for it expresses the idea of competitively self-assertive individuals, thereby presupposing a relatively equal power structure, and being at the outset less open to associational and collective values," in *The Politics of Community* (London: Harvester Wheatsheaf, 1993), 71. See also Carole Pateman, *The Sexual Contract* (Cambridge: Polity Press, 1988).

92. Gerald Dworkin, "Is More Choice Better Than Less?" in *The Theory and Practice of Autonomy*, Gerald Dworkin, ed. (Cambridge: Cambridge University Press, 1988), 62–84. My emphasis added.

93. Dworkin, 80. In the final chapter of *The Morality of Freedom* (Oxford: Clarendon Press, 1986), Joseph Raz also notes "meaningful" choice as an "adequate range of options" and not merely a quantity of options.

94. Dorothy Roberts, "The Genetic Tie," *University of Chicago Law Review* (1995): 209–39, 212. Also see Patricia Williams, "Reflections on Law, Contracts, and the Value of Life, " *Ms.* (May/June 1991): 42–46.

95. Zillah Eisenstein, *The Radical Future of Liberal Feminism* (Boston: Northeastern University Press, 1981). See also her *Feminism and Sexual Equality* (New York: Monthly Review Press, 1984).

96. Juliet Mitchell, "Women and Equality," in *Feminism and Equality*, Anne Phillips, ed. (New York: New York University Press, 1987), 24–43, 25. bell hooks, "Feminism: A Movement to End Sexist Oppression," in *Feminism and Equality*, Anne Phillips, ed. (New York: New York University Press, 1987), 62–76.

97. J. F. Childress, "The Body as Property: Some Philosophical Reflections," in *Transplantation Proceedings* 24 (October 1992): 2145.

98. Heidi Hartman, "Capitalism, Patriarchy and Job Segregation by Sex," in *The Signs Reader: Women, Gender and Scholarship*, Elizabeth Abel and Emily K. Abel, eds. (Chicago: University of Chicago Press, 1983). See also the works of Michéle Barrett and Sheila Rowbotham listed in the bibliography.

99. Patricia Williams, "Reflections on Law, Contracts, and the Value of Life, " *Ms.* (May/June 1991): 42–46, 43.

100. Brill, xiii.

101. Contemporary Aristotelian Hannah Arendt accepts this hierarchy of public

over private life and argues that the private life constitutes deprivation of glory. "Privacy literally means being deprived of something . . . men who live private lives are similar to slaves—not permitted to enter the public realm, and barbarians—choosing not to establish such a realm." To live a private life means forfeiture of citizenship, the good life, and, thus, justice. Hannah Arendt, *The Human Condition* (Chicago: University of Chicago Press, 1958), 17, 58.

102. Copelon, 33. See also Frances Olsen, "Constitutional Law: Feminist Critiques of the Public/Private Distinction," *Constitutional Commentary* (1993): 319–27.

103. Joan Williams, "Gender Wars: Selfless Women in the Republic of Choice," *New York University Law Review* (1991): 1559–1633, 1562.

104. Sheila Rowbotham, *Woman's Consciousness, Man's World* (Harmondsworth: Penguin, 1973). Catharine MacKinnon, *Fem., Marx., Method.*

105. Rowbotham, 10. Simone de Beauvoir also advocates independent self-realization as an integral part of women's liberation. However, she argues that this epiphany is attained through women's entry into the workforce.

106. While comparing class and gender oppression may seem much like equating apples and watermelons, MacKinnon does see labor exploitation and sexual domination as analogous. She writes, "Sexuality is to feminism what labor is to Marxism," recognizing the need for collective self-realization as a requisite for emancipation. Michéle Barrett also writes about the usefulness of Marx's theory of alienation for feminism:

> Marx's theory of alienation is effective as a general theory of oppression and liberation for the reason that it has a strong relational character. It enables us to understand oppression not as an arbitrary imposition but as a process involving the oppressed. . . . Feminist theory and practice has tended to emphasize the necessity of engaging with subjectivity and consciousness as well as with external structures and it has attempted analysis of how an oppressed group comes to live out the dynamics of oppression in forms of collusion.

Michéle Barrett, "Marxist-Feminism and the Work of Karl Marx," in *Feminism and Equality*, Anne Phillips, ed. (New York: New York University Press, 1987), 44–61, 51–52.

107. Judith Jarvis Thompson, "A Defense of Abortion," *Philosophy and Public Affairs* (Princeton University Press, 1971), 47–66.

108. Alison Jaggar, "Political Philosophies of Women's Liberation," in *Feminism and Philosophy,* Mary Vetterling-Braggin, Frederick Elliston, and Jane English, eds. (Totowa, N.J.: Rowman and Allanheld, 1977).

109. Purdy, *Reproducing Persons,* 159.

110. Kristin Luker, *Abortion and the Politics of Motherhood* (Berkeley: University of California Press, 1984), 92.

111. Zillah Eisenstein, Feminism and Sexual Equality (New York: Monthly Review

Press, 1989), 13 (it takes the promise of individual equality and extends it to women as a sexual class).

112. Joan Williams, "Deconstructing Gender," in *Feminist Jurisprudence*, Patricia Smith, ed. (New York: Oxford University Press, 1993), 531–59, 550–51.

6

PRAXIS FEMINISM

*T*he preceding chapters constructed and explored various feminist responses to technological intervention in the womb, ultimately pointing out the inadequacy of univocal assessments of both technology and women.

With respect to technology, technophiles' eulogy of it and privacy advocates' blind acceptance of it ignore the ugly realities of current (and future?) administration and development of technology (concerns emphasized by FINRRAGE). Similarly superficial, technophobes dismiss the very idea of intervention, science, and consumerism as inherently patriarchal, regardless of the particular invention in question.

The technophilic, technophobic, and FINRRAGE approaches depend upon unrealistic conceptions of women, while the privacy pundits recognize individualism at the expense of gender. No feminist theory presented thus far has accounted for the real implications of gender, race, class, and social reality. Consequently, "women," a diverse group of females existing in our social reality, have yet to receive serious scrutiny. The need remains for a feminist response to technological intervention in the womb that is praxis-oriented in its assessment of both women and technology.

This chapter explores a few attempts to understand and assess both reproductive technology and women in social context, describing "praxis feminisms," assigning a possible legal framework to this feminist perspective and examining some of the potential problems associated with it.

Materialist Feminisms as Praxis-Oriented

Linda Gordon argues in *Woman's Body, Woman's Right* that the history of the birth control movement in the United States is the story of changing social relations, not developing technologies. Tracing the origins of the sponge to the ancient Jews, pessaries to the Egyptians (who used crocodile dung), and the condom to Fallopius in 1564, Gordon argues that birth control has always existed; minor improvements have been made, but the only real change surrounding birth control is public sentiment. She contends that it is social relations and dominant ideologies that assign historical meaning to birth control; political sentiment is socially, not technologically, determined.[1] Moreover, political sentiment is dynamic. For example, abortion had not been deemed a crime in the United States, or even a sin, until after 1869 when Pope Pius IX declared all terminations immoral, recommending excommunication.[2] Although abortion existed as common practice before Christ in Sumatra, Egypt, Israel, and India, Pope Pius' proclamation inspired anti-abortion feeling and laid the groundwork for restrictive legislation like the Comstock Laws, which prohibited contraception and dissemination of information about contraception.[3] Gordon's central thesis is that, while birth control itself has changed very little, the acceptance of birth control has fluctuated as a function of historical context. Changing social relations and dominant ideologies have affected the social meaning of birth control devices. Simply, technologies are neutral objects whose political acceptance or rejection (meaning) is a function of their present historical and social context.

To what do I refer when I cite the "historical and social context" of technology, for example? In a law review article titled, "In Context," Martha Minow and Elizabeth Spelman determine that "context" can refer to the demographics of the particular creator of an idea (for example, the individual framers of the Constitution), the demographics of the people interpreting the idea (the Supreme Court justices), or the particular structures, power relationships, and demographics of the present historical moment.[4] Consider the layered "context" of any given technological intervention in the womb. Who created it? Who uses it? How is it obtained? How much does it cost? Gordon maintains that it is not the exact scraps of plastic or combination of potions that politicize a given technology, but the answers to these questions of context that shape any technology as the friend or foe of women.

Interested in analyzing and defending a woman's right to safe and legal abortion against a hostile cultural backdrop, Rosalind Pollack Petchesky is not enthusiastic about the potential for success under the auspices of a civil-liberties struggle for privacy. The social realities of these technologies are never confronted by the "right to choose" approach—nor does flatly banning or embracing all technology provide solace.

In addition to recognizing the social situation of technology, Petchesky recognizes women as females constructed by our particular social existence. For Petchesky, "women" refers not only to individuals deserving maximum choice, but to people who are confronted with months of medical visits, constant urination, hormonal changes, and the primary responsibility for childbirth and rearing,[5] all of which may interfere with the ability to go to school, earn a living, and participate in society as an equal entity.[6] Thus, Petchesky not only believes in a constructed meaning of technology, but also of women's bodies:

> It is important to keep in mind that women's reproductive situation is never the result of biology alone, but of biology mediated by social and cultural organization.[7]

In contrast to the radical feminists who directly connect sex and gender and also the individualists who deny the importance of gender, Petchesky insists on the impact of social relations on the construction of gender categories.

Because Petchesky integrates the importance of social construction with the material reality of sexual difference, I refer to her as a materialist feminist. This cultural-social-contextual-interpretivist feminist view of the world is much like the radical social constructionist view I described in chapters 2 and 3. However, materialist feminisms do not resort to inevitabilities or sexual binaries; women are not born X and men Y, but rather we are all born a certain sex and are socially constructed accordingly.[8] Changing the basic structures of society—education, the law, the family—must occur in order to dramatically change the political, social, and economic situation of women. Materialist feminists like Petchesky have bridged the supposed gap between sameness and difference feminist theories by embracing understandings of women shaped by social reality. Petchesky recognized the inadequacy of both the individualist (privacy) and protectionist (essentialist) understandings of women and abortion:

> [O]ne group of feminists fought to expose and regulate the dangers to women in the trafficking and exploitation of their bodies, their need for protection, while others foresaw the dangers of protection, its tendency to be used as a pretext for denying women their capacity to be sexual, to work, or even to walk on the street. . . . Neither individualism—formulated as the 'right to privacy' in liberal constitutional tradition—nor paternalism has ever provided adequate solutions to women's collective oppression.[9]

Petchesky seeks an alternative to the individualist vs. radical debate by looking for a social understanding of both women and reproduction. By viewing women as they are situated here and now, materialist feminism is "less likely to be embarrassed by the occasional material importance of sex differences, while being equally vigilant against attempts to construct differences as 'neutral' or 'biological.' "[10]

Emphasizing the importance of the basic structures of society in socializing females as oppressed women, materialist feminism is a cousin of Marxism. I do not mean to imply that all materialist feminists recognize a single oppressed class and a ruling class, merely substituting women for the proletariat. Indeed, most materialist feminists recognize many oppressed classes because great attention is given to the plethora of real differences among women.[11] Materialist feminisms recognize the basic structures of society—law, education, family, and so on—as oppressive socializing forces. This recognition of society as pervasively flawed such that social revolution as opposed to mere political emancipation is required can be recognized as a relative of Marxism, as noted by Michéle Barrett.[12]

For example, Catharine MacKinnon presents a particular brand of materialist feminism that she calls "dominance."[13] Taking social construction seriously, MacKinnon doesn't view women as either genderless individuals or a single class of biologically determined females. Since men created the institutions, television, laws, magazines, and other cultural vestiges that shape us, our existence in their male-dominated society is oppressive. Contrary to privacy feminists' views, gender matters. And contrary to radical feminists, domination of women need not be experienced the same by all women, nor is this oppression inevitable; liberation can be accomplished when diverse women transcend alienation (another Marxist notion), gain collective consciousness, and subvert the current power structure. MacKinnon's view (and materialist feminism more generally) should be thought of as a separate inquiry from questions of sameness or difference. First, she argues that these conceptual categories are irrelevant: "In rape crisis centers, battered women's shelters, incest support groups, and organizations of former prostitutes against prostitution, for example, nobody experiences anything so taxonomic and generic and neutral and analytic and abstract and empty as sameness and difference."[14] Second, she contends that sameness and difference theories actually represent adherence to the same oppressive gender dualism. Simply, neither theory transcends this odious binary.

> Concealed is the substantive way in which man has become the measure of all things. Under the sameness standard, women are measured according to correspondence with man, our equality judged by our proximity to his measure. Under the difference standard, women are measured according to our lack of correspondence from man, our womanhood judged by our distance from his measure. Gender neutrality is the male standard, and the special protection rule is the female standard. Masculinity or maleness is the referent for both.[15]

Because materialist feminisms accept the diversity that characterizes women and, yet, create a transcendent theory of gender oppression and liberation, materialist feminisms are forms of praxis feminism. Praxis feminism refers to a type of feminist methodology that combines respect for consistent philosophy and the reality of women's situation: theory and practice. In an effort to illustrate the praxis nature of materialist feminisms, it is useful to explore various

119

materialist feminist responses to technological intervention in the womb.

Materialist Feminist Responses to Technological Intervention in the Womb

This section highlights three particular materialist feminist arguments as they relate to technological intervention in the womb. It is important to note that none of the three praxis feminists presented is necessarily mutually exclusive. I narrate these three viewpoints to suggest the richness of materialist feminism, though there are certainly more theories that I might have highlighted.[16]

First, Petchesky argues that because abortion can curb the physical and social implications of a woman's fertility—the sex-specific basis of women's oppression—it must be made available to all women.

> Rather than apologize for abortion, feminists must proclaim loudly . . . that access to safe, funded abortion is a positive social need of all women of childbearing age. Abortion is a necessary, though far from sufficient, condition of women's essential right and need, not only for bodily health and determination, but also for control over their work, their sexuality, and their relations with others—including existing children. From this perspective, abortion conducted under safe, affordable, and stigma-free conditions is neither a necessary evil nor a matter of private choice. Rather, it is a positive benefit that society has an obligation to provide to all who seek it, just as it provides education and health benefits.[17]

This is the crux of Petchesky's argument: she understands access to safe, legal, affordable abortion for all women as a prerequisite for equal political, social, and economic participation. In a society that claims to value equal citizenship regardless of race, age, sex, and so on, while inadequate contraception, unequal pay, and gender-specific responsibility for childbirth and rearing persist, it is not only ethical, but also necessary, to provide access to abortion.[18]

Following Petchesky's requirement for abortion provision as a positive social need for women, other feminists posit similar materialist feminist views of women and reproduction. Calling for provision of abortion as a social right, Rhonda Copelon has written several articles referring to abortion as an important facet of a woman's "affirmative right to self-determination."[19] Like Petchesky, Copelon insists upon universal access regardless of age or income and is quite critical of the privacy doctrine because negative rights to be free from the state do not provide meaningful choices to whole groups of women on the basis of class, age, geographic location, and so on. Drucilla Cornell dedicates an entire chapter to explaining her argument for women's access to abortion as a function of bodily integrity that is intimately required for individuation in a sea of social and symbolic recognitions.[20]

While these Petcheskyesque arguments recognize unwanted pregnancy as having grave social implications affecting the future of a woman's life, MacKinnon suggests that feminists should look "backward" to the social arrangements that condition women's pregnancies. MacKinnon contends that feminists should "start earlier"—instead of focusing on pregnancy itself, feminists should look at the conditions under which women became pregnant.[21] She argues, "If women are not socially accorded control over sexual access to their bodies, they cannot control much else about them."[22] MacKinnon is saying that because of the treatment of the sexes in reproduction—women are rarely in control of the circumstances that cause pregnancy—women are owed abortion as a sort of compensation or means of correcting the elemental injustice of sexual discrimination (domination).[23] To MacKinnon, women's control of their bodies is a powerful means of subverting or undermining this male domination. It is particularly because women's fertility is conditioned by social arrangements over which women have very little control that "access to abortion is necessary for women to survive [these] unequal social circumstances. . . . Because motherhood without choice is a sex equality issue, legal abortion should be a sex equality right."[24] Reva Siegel echoes this situated view of reproduction, arguing that a major flaw in the Supreme Court reasoning about reproduction is that the Court has continually held reproduction to be a physiological process rather than a social activity. Siegel argues:

Social forces play a powerful part in shaping the process of reproduction. Social forces define the circumstances under which a woman conceives a child, including how voluntary her participation in intercourse may be. Social forces determine whether a woman has access to methods of preventing and terminating a pregnancy, and whether it is acceptable for her to use them. Social forces determine the quality of health care available to a woman during pregnancy, and they determine whether a pregnant woman will be able to support herself throughout the term of gestation, or instead be forced to depend on others for support. Social relations determine who cares for a child once it is born, and what resources, rewards, and penalties attend the work of gestating and nurturing human life.[25]

A third materialist feminist, Ruth Colker, argues that feminists (and Supreme Court justices) should view reproduction with an eye toward health. According to Colker they should consider the full consequences of a woman's reproductive capacity—the nature of the activity, the use and availability of contraception, the availability of pre- and postnatal care, and so on.[26] Clearly, Colker takes an expansive, holistic view of what reproductive health entails. We might say Colker's "health" not only refers to the mere physiological process, but also to the general well-being of women. Like MacKinnon, she is uninterested in questions of sameness and difference. Colker looks at the real situation of women—for example, pregnant adolescents—and argues that a lack of reproductive health care dramatically affects their lives.

Perhaps the clearest example of how legal and available technology can drastically enrich women's health and social status is the history of illegal abortion. The fatal implications of illegal abortion were demonstrated in the United States before the *Roe* decision in 1973.[27] Unable to receive legal termination services, women resorted to self-inflicted miscarriages or "back-alley abortions." Many women suffered infection and consequent infertility, and some women died.[28]

One must merely look to countries that have stringent anti-abortion statutes and, consequently, high mortality rates from botched termination procedures to recognize the implications of illegal abortion. For example, until November 1996, South Africa had a severely restrictive abortion law that permitted early terminations in extreme circumstances only. In 1994, the Medical Research Council of South Africa, a non-political organization, published a study of fifty-five government hospitals throughout South Africa that estimated that nearly forty-five thousand women presented themselves to hospitals with complications from "incomplete" abortions annually. These documented women are the ones who actually made it to a hospital. Others went to private gynecologists or clinics. Those with enough money traveled abroad for safe, legal abortions. And many women—especially in rural areas—died without being admitted to a hospital.[29] Consequently, the Reproductive Rights Alliance estimates that close to 250,000 illegal abortions occurred each year. African National Congress (ANC) support for the Choice of Termination of Pregnancy Bill of 1996 was largely due to the severe health implications of restricted abortion that were documented by this Medical Research Council study. (The Choice of Termination of Pregnancy Act took effect in January 1997.)

Also consider Romania. Under Ceausescu and the restrictive reproductive health policies enforced between 1966 and 1989, maternal mortality reached heights unprecedented in Europe. The maternal mortality rate rose from 85 deaths per 100,000 live births in 1965, to 170 in 1983 (by contrast the number in the United States in 1996 was eight). Illegal and unsafe abortions accounted for more than 80 percent of maternal deaths between 1980 and 1989. In 1989, at least 445 deaths were attributable to illegal abortions.[30] Consequently, one of the first acts of the new transitional government was to remove the restrictions on the sale of contraceptives and to legalize abortion. In 1995 the number of deaths from illegal abortion was reduced to fifty-nine, and eighty-four women died in childbirth.[31] Clearly the numbers of casualties are still high. However, these figures do demonstrate that the situation is (if slowly) improving. (Note another parallel with South Africa: newly democratic governments recognizing women's health as an important element of social change.)

The health risks associated with illegal abortion particularly affect lower income women, young women, and women of color. In a history of black women and abortion, Loretta Ross explains that access to family planning is a necessary component of respectability, self-determination, and basic health.[32] Connie Chan regards reproductive control via legal and available technology a necessary condition for Asian-American women's survival:

> We need to insure that the issue is an essential item on the Asian-American political agenda. It is not a woman's issue; it is a community issue. . . . We can and must lead the Asian-American communities to recognize the importance . . . for the survival of these communities.[33]

While abortion may be the most notable technology fomenting women's health and social status, other reproductive technologies have contributed as well. For example, pregnant women are less likely to die from childbirth today than in 1925.[34] Although this statistic has been attributed to lower birth rates, better diet, and less stressful lifestyles, reproductive technologies have also promoted women's reproductive health and, thus, tempered the physical and social implications of pregnancy and birth.

A narrow birth canal, small bone structure, or awkward fetal positioning once meant that the chances of survival for both mother and child were slim. However, Cesarean sections are now a simple, routine procedure that magnifies those chances. Anesthesia is heralded as rescuing women from pain. Prenatal technologies such as amniocentesis, ultrasound, and other forms of early screening help identify and prevent fatal ectopic pregnancies.[35] Simply, legal and accessible technological intervention in the womb can save women's lives and improve their mental and physical health.[36]

Consequently, these three materialist feminists focus on divergent social phenomena—the prerequisites for social and political equality, dominance, and health—yet are united because they are concerned with sex in social context and they seek to resolve the inequalities that exist as a result of socialization.

Does all this talk about equality suggest that women should be "equal to" men? Is using rights-based language not using the master's tools to disassemble the master's house? Equality analysis should not be mistakenly understood to "rest on any direct comparison of women with men." As Drucilla Cornell argues in *The Imaginary Domain*, "It undermines the full power of the equality appeal to

. . . seek to bring women 'up to' the position of men, rather than on an ethical conception of personhood that would demand a more egalitarian social order altogether."[37] If we understand Cornell's "individuation" as necessary for any meaningful concept of selfhood and any role in society as a contributing member, we accept the exigency of available contraception on demand. Alison Jaggar explains that the feminist call for equality is a "more determinate and substantive conception of equality, equality of outcome or condition rather than equality of procedure or opportunity."[38] Moreover, as praxis feminists, materialists do not assume a gender binary where one class could be matched with the other. Yet these materialist feminists do identify general proclivities. Marilyn Frye calls this "pattern perception":

> Patterns sketched in broad strokes make sense of our experiences, but it is not a single or uniform sense. They make our different experiences intelligible in different ways. Naming patterns is like charting the prevailing winds over a continent, which does not imply that every individual and item in the landscape is identically affected. . . . Our epistemological issues have to do with the strategies of discovering patterns and articulating them effectively, judging the strength and scope of patterns, understanding the variance of experience from what we take to be a pattern.[39]

In this sense, materialist feminists' claims of domination or lack of respect for women's health or women's social and political inferiority due to a lack of bodily autonomy are recognized as broadly systematic—as opposed to the atomized individualist view of privacy feminists or the strict universalistic view of radical feminists. Consequently, although materialist feminists do appeal to substantive values (such as equality or self-determination), this appropriation does not imply subscription to particular characterizations of women.

Some materialist feminist rhetoric sounds much like technophilia—understanding biology, mitigated by technology, as the answer to gender inequality. However, there are two main differences. First, technophiles blame reproductive biology for all gender inequities in society. They see a causal relationship between sexual difference and differential treatment, almost justifying such disparity. Con-

versely, the materialist feminists described in this chapter believe
that society has ascribed meaning to biology. MacKinnon, Siegel,
Cornell, Colker, Petchesky, and other praxis feminists understand
that women's oppression is not innate, but a function of (reversible/
changeable) social context. Consequently, technophiles and materialist feminists point to different sources of oppression: biology and
society, respectively. Regardless, their solution to women's oppression—legal and available technology—appears to be the same. Not
so. The second difference between technophiles and these materialists is that, while the former embrace the idea of technological intervention in the womb, the latter view bodily self-control as a result of
reproductive technology developed and administered under certain
conditions, which seems to make materialist feminists like FINR-
RAGE. Any feminist response to technological intervention in the
womb must respect the comments of FINRRAGE and other empiri-
cal studies that highlight the negative aspects of certain technologies
worldwide. Yet materialist feminists are hopeful about the positive
possibilities of technological intervention in the womb, if used and
developed under improved circumstances. Furthermore, materialist
feminists are praxis feminists who view women as a conglomerate
of diverse individuals, respecting the personal choices of women to
define their own selfhood. We can celebrate the differences among
women without deconstructing our collective conscious because we
share the desire to respect each other and to be respected as self-
defined women; the gender binary is replaced by multiple differences. As Cornell contends,

> This program is neither illiberal nor puritanical. It assumes no
> theoretical description of women as the truth of our sex. As a
> result, it does not encode any particular figure of woman as the
> basis of the demand of equality. The only restriction on the
> free play of our sexual imaginary is the respect for the equal
> worth of others in public space demanded by the degradation
> prohibition. This respect we owe one another.[40]

The Equal Protection Clause as a Legal
Materialist Praxis Feminism

Regardless of their particular version of materialist feminism, Petchesky, MacKinnon, Colker, and other praxis feminists have embraced

the Equal Protection Clause of the Constitution as a potential means of establishing an affirmative right to abortion based upon gender. Sylvia Law was one of the first to advocate this legal avenue in an article published in the *University of Pennsylvania Law Review* in 1984.[41] Frustrated with the sex-neutral or "assimilationist" constitutional sex-equality doctrine (privacy) because it ignored the realities of biological reproductive difference, Law sought "to create a stronger Constitutional concept of sex-based equality"[42]:

> Neither the assimilationist vision nor the respect-for-difference vision squarely confronts the problem of reconciling sexual equality with the reality of biological differences.[43]

Although she recognized the significance of sexual difference in society, she did not subscribe to radical feminist notions of separatism or special treatment. Rather, she hoped to negotiate biological difference within the traditional concepts of human freedom and equal opportunity. She argued that any just concept of citizenship had to be cognizant of the real implications of different reproductive biology:

> Pregnancy, abortion, reproduction, and creation of another human being are special—very special. Women have these experiences. Men do not. An equality doctrine that ignores the unique quality of these experiences implicitly says that women can claim equality only insofar as they are like men. . . . deny as we might, the reality remains that only women experience pregnancy. If women are to achieve fully equal status in American society, including sharing of power traditionally held by men, and retain control of their bodies, our understanding of sex equality must encompass a strong constitutional equality guarantee that requires radically increasing options available to each individual, and more importantly, allowing the human personality to break out of the present dichotomized system.[44]

Because the burden of pregnancy is felt unequally, a just society demands that the state not exaggerate this natural inequity by imposing the burden of unintended pregnancy upon women (that is, denying them the right to abortion), because it is a burden men can never bear. Just as Petchesky argues that lack of reproductive control limits women's ability to function as fully equal citizens, Law contends that the burden of sexual reproduction is leveled unequally upon women and the law must reflect this biological and social reality. Thus, she supports the right to abortion on the basis of the contextual meaning of sexual difference.

While Law presents a legal alternative to the sex-blind privacy approach to abortion rights, her intention is to highlight the legal injustice of the state prohibiting a woman from obtaining termination services on the basis of sexual difference. Although her motivations are more gender-sensitive than those of adherents to the privacy perspective, state neutrality may again be the outcome of such "state limitation" claims. However, this important exposition inspired a flood of articles advocating the use of the Equal Protection Clause to justify access for all women to termination-of-pregnancy services.[45]

Ratified on July 9, 1868, section one of the Fourteenth Amendment to the United States Constitution reads:

> All persons born or naturalized in the United States and subject to the jurisdiction thereof, are citizens of the United States and the State wherein they reside. No State shall make or enforce any law which shall abridge the privileges or immunities of citizens of the United States; nor shall any State deprive any person of life, liberty, or property, without due process of law; nor deny to any person within its jurisdiction the equal protection of these laws.

Although all citizens are owed equal protection of the laws, not all classifications receive heightened scrutiny. The amendment was passed in the wake of the Civil War, and, as constitutional law expert Gerald Gunther notes, "if the history and immediate purpose of the Fourteenth Amendment were all that counted, only racial classifications directed against blacks would be suspect."[46] Are women included in this category of "suspect classes"?

In one of the first Supreme Court cases on this issue, *Bradwell v. State* (1873), the Court used a very relaxed standard of review to uphold a law denying women the right to practice law.[47] In this early period, only two standards of review existed—relaxed and strict—and the latter was reserved almost exclusively for race-based discrimination cases. In the early 1970s, the Supreme Court adopted a heightened standard of scrutiny with respect to sex-based discrimination, still falling short of suspect classification (despite an eloquent argument by Justice Brennan in *Frontiero v. Richardson*).[48] It was a 1976 case, *Craig v. Boren,* concerning sex-specific alcohol age limits that provided Justice Brennan the opportunity to explicitly declare an intermediate standard of review.[49] Until recently, this intermediate standard of review had been applied to sex-discrimination cases. However, a well-publicized case regarding women's admission to an exclusively male military institute in Virginia may have finally placed gender within the elite category of "suspect" classifications deserving strict scrutiny. Delivering the majority opinion for the Supreme Court, Justice Ginsburg referred to Virginia's burden of demonstrating "an exceedingly persuasive justification for excluding women."[50] Although concurring in the judgment (striking down the policy as unjustified discrimination), Chief Justice Rehnquist expressed serious discontent over the establishment of this "exceedingly persuasive justification" standard.

> We have adhered to [the intermediate standard] ever since [*Craig v. Boren*]. While the majority adheres to this test today, it also says that the State must demonstrate an 'exceedingly persuasive justification' to support gender-based classifications. . . . To avoid introducing potential confusion, I would have adhered more closely to our traditional [standard] that a gender-based classification 'must bear a close and substantial relationship to important government objectives.'[51]

Is this tough review standard greater than the *Craig* intermediate review model such that it creates a fourth category of review? Or is an "exceedingly pursuasive justification" the same requirement as strict scrutiny? The answer is yet unclear. However, Justice Scalia's lengthy dissent explicitly accuses the majority of creating a "sweeping" standard of review for sex-based discrimination that is "indistinguishable from strict scrutiny."[52] Consequently, it appears that sex-based discrimination is perhaps now among the elite classifications receiving strict scrutiny review by the Supreme Court.

Keeping this (strict?) scrutiny standard in mind, there are divergent theoretical interpretations of the Equal Protection Clause, the anti-differentiation and anti-subordination perspectives. Advocates of the former assert that it is "inappropriate to treat individuals differently on the basis of race or sex because of a stereotyped view of their race or sex-based abilities."[53] Colker explains that this outlook is essentially individualistic for two reasons: "First, it focuses on the motivation of the individual institution that has allegedly discriminated without attention to the larger societal context in which the institution operates. Second, it focuses on the specific effect of the alleged discrimination on discrete individuals rather than on groups."[54] Because anti-differentiation advocates promote the equality of individuals regardless of the historical status and present social context of their demographic group, no deference is given to the implications of gender. Paradoxically, gender blindness and color blindness must be observed. For example, a white man has the legal standing to file a discrimination suit if a less qualified woman or non-white person receives preferential treatment and is hired over him, because the anti-differentiation perspective is not concerned with redistributing power among social groups, but rather with guaranteeing procedural fairness among individuals. All demographic membership—regardless of the power or subordination associated with such characteristics—must be ignored according to the anti-differentiation perspective.

In contrast to advocates of the former position, anti-subordination advocates are sensitive to the social context of people. The anti-subordination perspective "seeks to eliminate the power disparities between men and women and between whites and non-whites, through the development of laws and policies that directly address those disparities."[55] Anti-subordination scrutiny requires examining and then rectifying the real social impact of seemingly neutral laws. J. Ralph Lindgren succinctly argues for this antisubordination interpretation of the Equal Protection Clause as a more useful grounds for understanding reproduction:

Withholding RU 486 from the American market appears to have nothing to do with gender. Gender does not appear in the statement of the regulation or the description of the practice. It looks innocent. But, when one considers that restriction in the concrete context of the biological, sociological and moral differences [disparately felt by men and women], these restrictions look quite different. We then see that . . . the procedure is biased, i.e. the burdens and benefits allocated by the restrictions are not distributed randomly among women and men. The procedure disproportionately burdens women. We also see that these restrictions magnify the burdens already imposed by biology, social structure and mores on women, all relative to the advantage of men.[56]

This approach recognizes that all people are not functionally equal in a society that historically harbors sexual and racial hierarchy. Therefore, anti-subordination advocates encourage race and sex-specific redress, most notably in the form of affirmative-action policies. Colker argues that the anti-subordination approach should be used to justify women's access to abortion because "if we are committed to women moving toward their aspirations for their authentic self, then we need to avoid coercing women to enter a deeply gendered role."[57] Access to birth control is understood to afford women control of their biological selves and social lifestyles, conditions of equal citizenship; therefore, these services must be provided to all who need them.

Problems with the Equal Protection Framework

There are two potential problems with using the Equal Protection Clause to assess all reproductive technologies.

First, the equality approach to abortion rights simply has not proved judicially successful. Three hurdles stand between equality advocates and Supreme Court recognition of exceedingly heightened scrutiny for regulation and administration of technological intervention in the womb under the Equal Protection Clause: (1) the legacy of *Geduldig*, (2) the legacy of *Feeney*, and (3) political efficacy.

In *Geduldig v. Aiello*, the Supreme Court reviewed a California state policy of excluding pregnancy from disability insurance. Despite common sense, the Court rejected the notion that discrimination against pregnant women constitutes sex-based discrimination, instead adopting a view that pregnant as opposed to non-pregnant persons (rather than women) were targeted by the law.[58] Consequently, even if sex-based discrimination were to be reviewed under strict scrutiny, pregnancy-related cases might not be deemed sex-based discrimination. In response to *Geduldig* and other decisions that narrowly construed pregnancy as outside the boundaries of sex-based discrimination, Congress passed the Pregnancy Discrimination Act of 1978 to ensure insurance coverage of pregnancy-related medical expenditures. Although with this measure, "a cardinal difference between the sexes became an invalid reason for disadvantaging women,"[59] the act explicitly denied that failure to fund abortion could constitute pregnancy discrimination.[60] Thus, after *Geduldig* and considering the exception to the Pregnancy Discrimination Act, to suggest that abortion restraints constitute *per se* sex discrimination requires arguing against precedent. Reva Siegel, Frances Olsen, Anita Allen, and others have pointed to language in the *Thornburgh, Webster,* and *Casey* decisions suggesting an increasing understanding of reproductive control as containing a gender dimension.[61] Consider Justice O'Connor's discussion of women's "unique" reproductive liberty, a necessary prerequisite for women to "participate equally in the economic and social life of the Nation."[62] In fact, Justice O'Connor's plurality opinion in *Casey* is full of language about the unique situation of pregnant women. In addition, although he is now retired from the bench, Justice Blackmun's opinion explicitly mentioned the applicability of the Fourteenth Amendment due to the gender-bias of motherhood. Consequently, perhaps the Supreme Court is ready to overrule its quirky decision that laws concerning pregnancy are not sufficiently sex-based to be reviewed by the Equal Protection Clause as sexual discrimination.

Second, the Supreme Court has repeatedly required plaintiffs to meet a difficult standard of proving legislative intent. In *Personnel Administrator v. Feeney*, the Supreme Court considered the constitutionality of a Massachusetts law granting "absolute lifetime" preference to veterans for civil-service jobs. Although the statute was enacted before women were eligible for most civil-service jobs, the Court found that creating benefits for veterans was not motivated by a discriminatory purpose, since veteran/non-veteran distinctions are not explicitly gender-based; the Court found no *per se* sex-discrimination. Moreover, the Court examined the intentions of the legislature in determining that the neutral-on-its-face statute did not have an adverse effect that reflected "invidious gender-based discrimination."[63] This latter criterion (if it can be at all distinguished from the former) has proved almost impossible to meet, because a smoking gun demonstrating a desire to cause harm is rarely discoverable.[64]

Ruth Colker suggests that a more appropriate construction of the "intent inquiry" should not look to explicit and conscious discriminatory purpose (even Jesse Helms refrains from providing a smoking gun like "let's keep women barefoot and pregnant"), but that the disproportionate impact of facially neutral statutes should also be considered under the rubric of discriminatory intent. "Thus, the appropriate doctrinal question should be whether a legislature would have been willing to impose these kinds of burdens on women if it fully considered their well-being."[65] Reva Siegel also suggests a refined standard of intent. She says the appropriate framework for assessing legislative intent is to ask if "but for certain stereotypical assumptions about women, a legislature may not view coercing women to perform the work of motherhood as a reasonable way of promoting the welfare of the unborn."[66]

Third, it is questionable whether advocating "women's equality" as opposed to the more neutral-sounding "privacy" is efficacious. (Of course, feminists should not necessarily restrict themselves to advocating the pragmatic rather than the desirable.) However, it may now be possible to discuss reproduction in a gendered manner, as a social activity rather than a physiological process shrouded in the private realm.

Relying on the Fourteenth Amendment has gained public momentum following Ruth Bader Ginsburg's Supreme Court confirmation hearing in 1993.

Prior to her nomination, Ginsburg had discussed her views on using the equality approach to safeguard provision of abortion in several law review articles and speeches that reached limited audiences. As early as 1984 (around the same time as publication of the Sylvia Law article), in an address before the University of North Carolina School of Law, Ginsburg contended that abortion regulations affect "a woman's autonomous charge of her full life's course . . . her ability to stand in relation to man, society, and the state as an independent, self-sustaining equal citizen."[67] Only months before her testimony began, she delivered a now well-known lecture, stating that *Roe* should have "homed in more precisely on the woman's equality dimension of the issue . . . [since] disadvantageous treatment of a woman because of her pregnancy and reproductive choice is a paradigm case of discrimination on the basis of sex."[68]

Due to the political nature of abortion and the precedent of asking nominees their views on abortion (well established by the Bork confirmation hearings), it was likely that Ginsburg would have been asked about abortion during her Supreme Court confirmation hearings even if she had no 'paper trail' regarding the subject. However, the fact that she was well-published in this area meant that such inquiries were even more likely—perhaps even justified—and specific.

Although throughout the hearings, she clearly supported the notion that a general, unenumerated right to privacy exists, and that this right protects a woman's right to choose abortion, she also discussed the "equality" aspect of reproductive freedom:

> *Senator Feinstein:* If I understand what you are saying—correct me if I am wrong—you are saying that *Roe* could have been decided on Equal Protection grounds rather than the fundamental right to privacy.
> *Judge Ginsburg:* Yes, Senator, except in one respect. I never made it either/or. . . . I have always said both, that the equal-protection strand should join together with the autonomy-of-decision-making strand; so that it wasn't a question of equal protection or personal autonomy, it was a question of both.[69]

On national television, Ginsburg contended that abortion is both a function of individual autonomy and a necessary element of women's equality with men. In addition to genuinely believing these two principles to be complementary, Ginsburg demonstrated her "commitment to gradual change and her respect for the political process"[70] in her remarks. By advocating legal reform rather than legal revolution, she not only proved herself politically savvy, she fostered mainstream acceptance of the equality perspective.

Ginsburg's testimony highlights another important feature of the equality perspective worth noting. Although this chapter presents the equal protection approach as separate from the privacy perspective explained in the previous chapter, they are not necessarily wholly distinct concepts. Anita Allen argues that endorsement of the Equal Protection Clause can be either "additive" or "fixative."[71] She describes the latter (where my arguments seem to be located) in the following manner: "The fixative perspective contends that Equal Protection Clause argument could salvage the constitutional case for reproductive rights; privacy jurisprudence should yield to a conceptually, jurisprudentially, and politically superior Equal Protection alternative."[72] Although I do believe that the Equal Protection Clause is a more appropriate place to ground reproductive law and policy, it is inaccurate to characterize promotion of the Equal Protection Clause as "fixative" because this implies a "clean swap": equality replacing privacy. As mentioned, patrons of the Equal Protection Clause and praxis feminists more generally include promotion of self-determination and choice as central features of their advocacy. Similar to privacy feminists' reverence for choice and self-determination in the name of individual rights, praxis-materialist feminist advocacy of the Equal Protection Clause includes respect for choice and self-determination in the name of women; to subvert dominance and as a prerequisite for equal participation in society as social, political, and economic equals, women need reproductive choice. The point is not that feminists should drop promotion of choice and self-determination altogether; rather, that these are important elements of women's struggle for equality and should be understood within this context. In other words, because similar virtues are valued, even the supposedly fixative approach is largely additive.

Regardless of how we characterize promotion of the Equal Protection Clause, Supreme Court developments and Ginsburg's successful confirmation suggest that the equality perspective may be politically viable. Consequently, the few structural problems with the equality perspective may not be problems at all.[73]

The second potential problem with using the equality perspective to respond to all technological intervention in the womb is a theoretical concern. Petchesky, Copelon, Law, and Colker all discuss the sexual-social relationship between sex-equality and abortion (or, at most, contraception), but can this approach be used to assess technological intervention in the womb more generally? Petchesky specifically renounces inclusion of other reproductive technologies in the concluding remarks to her book:

> The 'right to have children' and the 'right not to have them' are not equivalent rights . . . these two dimensions of reproductive politics and life-activity involve qualitatively distinct problems. . . . To construct a false equation between them suggests a market model of 'reproductive rights' in which 'choices' are a grab bag of discrete personal desires. . . . All that a politics of reproduction is concerned with, in this view, is allowing individuals to 'maximize' their desires.[74]

Petchesky argues that the cultural interpretation of fertility and infertility technologies is not only different, but opposed. While abortion allows women to assert their independence from biological destiny and cultural expectation, IVF reinforces motherhood as "normal" or at least desirable, perpetuating the idea of a maternal instinct or innate need for women to be pregnant, soccer moms. Abortion allows women to defy tradition and biological destiny, while infertility technologies supposedly reinforce such norms. Furthermore, because Petchesky perceives fertility control as a function of social equality for women, not individual liberty, she insists that blending all reproductive options amounts to a struggle for reproductive freedom, a struggle within the realm of civil liberties. In other words, my holistic approach is ideologically incapable of being compatible with a discussion of gender equality. She suggests that conflating all forms of technological intervention in the womb to be a single entity of feminist inquiry is ideologically aligned with discussion of individual rights, which is different from a discussion of gender equality.

> [E]quality doctrine doesn't demand that women be allowed to choose to have abortions because women are entitled to be treated with autonomy. Instead, it insists that women be allowed to choose to have abortions because of women's position in society—the roles and responsibilities of women in society in relation to others.[75]

However, I contend that access to other reproductive technologies is also part of women's struggle for equality for three reasons.

First, these technologies redefine who is a mother. When lesbians, single women, and sixty-three-year-old women conceive and give birth, new definitions of motherhood are created. With the assistance of these technologies, many women have been able to re-create reproduction in their own vision, apart from male dominance and the stereotype Petchesky seeks to avoid.

Second, it is impossible to separate women's struggle for bodily self-determination from the struggle for gender equality. The bottom line is that these technologies are about women gaining control over their futures. If technological intervention in the womb is available under certain conditions, it is a form of metaphysical control, as not only the body, but also one's destiny is tamed. All forms of reproductive technology—those surrounding infertility, prenatal development, and birth—are mechanisms that can afford women greater health and control if developed, allocated, and administered in a fashion that is sensitive to the real condition of women in society. Thanks to such mitigated reproductive technology, women are not slaves to their biology, whether fertile or infertile. This sexual self-determination is a facet of sexual equality because reproduction is sex-specific.

Only women become pregnant as a result of rape and incest. Only women have unintended pregnancies. Because potential life develops within the confines of a woman's body, only women confront inevitable weight gain and contractions. It is women's bodies that undergo amniocentesis and ultrasound. It is women who are branded "barren," like a plot of land that will not bear fodder, while men are lovingly called "bachelors" or clinically termed "sterile."[76] Whether childbirth is "natural" or managed in any form, all children are of woman born. This struggle for sexual self-determination and health is deeply sex-specific, as all women potentially face aspects of sexual reproduction and men do not in the same way. Thus, sexual self-determination is an important facet of gender liberation.

Third, recognizing pregnancy-inducing technologies under the same framework as pregnancy-inhibiting technologies requires deconstructing classic understandings of sexuality, parenthood, the family, and the state, a project materialist feminists embrace.

Petchesky's distinction between the fertile and infertile promotes what I call *the polarization of motherhood*. This is the idea that non-motherhood issues are somehow more feminist than motherhood issues. For the last two decades, feminist organizations working both inside and outside the political structure have pushed for recognition of a myriad of "women's issues." Abortion rights are perhaps the most visible. However, women in the military, sexual harassment, homophobia, and affirmative-action hiring practices have also characterized recent activism. In an article in *The Guardian* that argued that "the feminist record on motherhood is pretty appalling—and that is putting it politely," Maureen Freely contended "the major feminist issues of the nineties are date rape and menopause—issues that concern women before they settle down and have children and after the children have left."[77] What about subsidized day care? Pay for housewives? Prenatal care? The list of "women's issues" conspicuously ignores "mothering issues."[78]

Meanwhile, at the 1992 Republican convention, Marilyn Quayle, Pat Buchanan, Pat Robertson, and other members of the right wing repeatedly used the term "family values" as they glorified the 1950s notion of women baking cookies in the kitchen. Their extreme rhetoric, coupled with the birth-blind activism of women's groups and the Democratic Party, conceived a political polarization of motherhood; while the women's movement and the Democratic Party championed women's control over their occupations, lifestyles, and bodies, the Republican Party cornered the market on birth.

Thus, in recent years, giving birth and becoming pregnant have been (falsely) construed as conservative matters. Campaign pollsters in both 1992 and 1996 noted that voters who knew Hillary Clinton had a child were more eager to support the Clintons than voters who were unaware of this fact. Hillary's role as a mother made her palatable to those otherwise intimidated by her strength and independence. Not surprising, it was after discovering this information in 1992 that Chelsea Clinton emerged and Tipper Gore, mother of four, began touring with Hillary. The 1996 campaign involved a similar scenario. In the same month as her independent political actions were being closely scrutinized in Washington, Hillary Clinton published a book on child-rearing called *It Takes a Village* and went on a nationwide book tour. Chelsea Clinton was increasingly visible—remember the image of Chelsea and her mother riding elephants together in Asia? The message from these campaigns?

Regardless of one's philosophy and actions, motherhood itself is viewed as inherently conservative.[79]

Pregnancy and birth can and should be reclaimed as realistic experiences of many women without heralding them as the central experiences that define us as women. Neither one's femininity nor feminism should be predicated upon whether or not one gives birth, allowing for a more inclusive definition of women and health. Feminists should champion menopause research and abortion rights as well as lesbian-parenting rights, prenatal care, and day care, because anything less is simply a repeat of politics as usual—dividing mothers and non-mothers (that is, all women), but also fostering a hierarchy of feminism, with some women being "more feminist" than others purely on the basis of their motherhood status. Similarly, we should not glorify natural childbirth as "more feminist" than medicated childbirth or natural conception as "more feminist" than assisted conception. Women's physical conditions and desires must not be construed in terms of healthy/unhealthy or feminist/unfeminist. The fact is that healthy women are a diverse conglomerate: some are pregnant and don't want to be, and others are unable to conceive and want to. Michelle Stanworth suggests that feminists should stop debating the parameters of what is natural and what is artificial, claiming one or the other is more feminist, and instead concentrate upon "creating the political and cultural conditions in which such technologies can be employed by women to shape the experience of reproduction according to their own definitions."[80] Reproductive health must be redefined, not in terms of productive ability but control in social context. The only common feature among women of various physical and emotional conditions is the univocal desire to affect the outcome of our existence. Again, this is not a call for individual self-determination, but survival in a society that requires bodily integrity as a prerequisite for equality.

> It is not rhetoric but reality to say that if we [women] can not control whether, when, and under what conditions we will have sex and children, there is little else in our lives that we can control.[81]

Consequently, if what is appealing about access to abortion is the deconstruction of social expectation and the establishment of equality, then we should recognize the even greater potential to subvert tradition via the total eradication of a polarized vision of women by construing women on a spectrum rather than at dichotomous poles, especially since many of the women using infertility technologies are lesbian, single, and/or older.

Finally, it should be reiterated that a holistic materialist feminist policy response to technological intervention in the womb based on praxis feminist methodology would not treat all individual technologies in a sweeping manner. Although we should respond to types of technological intervention in the womb under one overarching framework, each individual technology must be individually scrutinized against this umbrella criteria. For example, debate among feminists has ensued regarding support for RU 486.[82] Discussions among feminists about the implications of this abortificient or any particular technology would be facilitated by a common understanding of concerns and minimum standards. We should establish threshold criteria that all technological interventions in the womb must meet. Although infertility technologies and contraception should be judged by this comprehensive understanding, this does not presuppose that all individual technologies will be regarded in a like manner.

Conclusion

Materialist feminisms are praxis-oriented because they focus upon broad understandings of the vast category "women" in our social context. Moreover, in addition to being inclusive of all women, materialist feminisms consist of a mixture of other feminist paradigms. Like technophilia, materialist feminists find technological intervention in the womb to be a potential savior—though under just conditions of administration and development, as FINRRAGE feminists insist. Like the technophobes, materialists question social hierarchies and find power in gender. And, like the privacy feminist, materialist solutions focus upon legal strategy and political efficacy.

Notes

1. Linda Gordon, *Woman's Body, Woman's Right: Birth Control in America* (New York: Penguin, 1977). In chapter 4, I mentioned several feminist critiques of scien-

tific research and technological development that have exposed extensive male bias.

2. Until the 1869 Papal declaration *Apostolicae sedis*, abortion had been condoned until the point of "quickening." Different from viability, quickening is regarded as the moment when the fetus acquires a soul. Interestingly, Gordon notes that Aristotle, Hippocrates, and the Romans each set this point earlier for males than for females. Regardless, abortion before quickening was not a crime, not even a sin. Gordon, 52. For a complete history of abortion in the Catholic Church, consult the "Abortion in Good Faith" series published by Catholics for a Free Choice, 1436 U Street, N.W., Washington, D.C. 20009.

3. For an excellent discussion of this era, see Ellen Chesler, *Woman of Valor: Margaret Sanger and the Birth Control Movement in America* (New York: Simon and Schuster, 1992).

4. Martha Minow and Elizabeth Spelman, "In Context," *Southern California Law Review* (1990): 1597–1652.

5. The Census Bureau reported that one-third of all households in 1990 were headed by single mothers. U.S. Census Bureau, "The Statistics: Comparing the State of Children," 12 April 1994.

6. Rosalind Pollack Petchesky, *Abortion and Woman's Choice* (Boston: Northeastern University Press, 1984).

7. Petchesky, 6.

8. I regard Simone de Beauvoir as the mother of materialist feminism. She was one of the first to recognize the importance of social institutions like the family and work in creating females as the "other."

9. Petchesky, 191.

10. Jennifer Wicke, "Celebrity Material: Materialist Feminism and the Culture of Celebrity," *Materialist Feminism*, Toril Moi and Janice Radway, eds., *The South Atlantic Quarterly* (Fall 1994): 751–78, 759.

11. Interestingly, however, some materialist feminists do posit a coherent vision of the oppressor as a single class. For example, see Christine Littleton's explanation of "the male power system" as a "club." In "Reconstructing Sexual Equality," in *Feminist Jurisprudence*, Patricia Smith, ed. (New York: Oxford University Press, 1993), 110–36, 123–24 she notes

> countless examples of men lacking power—the soldier who does not choose his target, the assembly-line worker who does not control the product of his labor, the father who does not choose his absence from his children's lives, the lover who does not choose the image in his head that makes him so critical of his mate's shortcomings. . . . [But] individual or class differences among men in the degree of power they hold over women are not directly relevant to the issue of male power as a system. Rather, the form of male

power that constructs male dominance as a social system rather than as a systematic assertion of dominance by particular men can be viewed as concentrated in the hands of few men who are at or near the top of intersecting hierarchies of sex, race, and class, reserved to those in what I will call the *club*.

12. Michéle Barrett, "Marxist-Feminism and the Work of Karl Marx," *Feminism and Equality*, Anne Phillips, ed. (New York: New York University Press, 1987), 44–61.

13. Several of Catharine MacKinnon's publications are noted in the bibliography.

14. Catharine MacKinnon, "Reflections on Sex Equality Under Law," *Yale Law Journal* (1991): 1281–328, 1293. Hereafter, MacKinnon, *Reflections*. Also "Legal Perspectives on Sexual Difference," in *Theoretical Perspectives on Sexual Difference*, Deborah Rhode, ed. (New Haven: Yale University Press, 1990), 213–25 ("Social and political equality are lived-out social systems that are basically indifferent to abstract conceptual categories like sameness and difference."). Hereafter, MacKinnon, *Legal Perspectives*.

15. MacKinnon, *Legal Perspectives*, 217.

16. I suggest two others in particular. Drucilla Cornell, *The Imaginary Domain* (New York: Routledge, 1995) (outlining basic conditions that ensure a minimum degree of individuation, which is necessary for the equal chance to develop selfhood and participate in society as equal social and political beings). Christine Littleton, "Reconstructing Sexual Equality," in *Feminist Jurisprudence*, Patricia Smith, ed. (New York: Oxford University Press, 1993), 110–36 (arguing for an "acceptance" model of difference that denies biological-determinism, and seeks to eliminate the ways that difference is used to justify sex inequality).

17. Petchesky, 387.

18. Most technophiles and technophobes would also agree that safe, funded abortion should be made available. However, they might disagree with other aspects of Petchesky's argument.

19. Rhonda Copelon, "From Privacy to Autonomy," in *From Abortion to Reproductive Freedom: Transforming a Movement*, Marlene Gerber Fried, ed. (Boston: South End Press, 1990). See also "Unpacking Patriarchy: Reproduction, Sexuality, Originalism, and Constitutional Change," in *A Less than Perfect Union*, J. Lobel, ed. (New York: Monthly Review Press, 1988). "Beyond the Liberal Idea of Privacy: Toward a Positive Right of Autonomy," in *Judging the Constitution: Critical Essays on Judicial Lawmaking*, Michael W. McCann and Gerald L. Houseman, eds. (Glenview, Ill.: Scott Foresman and Co., 1989).

20. Cornell, 31.

21. MacKinnon, *Reflections*, 1312.

22. Catharine MacKinnon, "Toward Feminist Jurisprudence," *Feminist Jurispru-*

dence, Patricia Smith, ed. (New York: Oxford University Press, 1993), 610–20, 616. Hereafter, MacKinnon, *Toward a Feminist.* I understand this argument as parallel to classic affirmative action arguments where past injustice is rectified in the present.

23. MacKinnon's dominance theory is not necessarily pro-abortion. In one of her earlier articles, she lamented the availability of abortion as fomenting male domination because it makes sex more readily available to men. To this end, she noted that the Playboy Foundation had always been a big supporter of abortion rights. "In other words, under conditions of gender inequality, sexual liberation in this sense does not free women; it frees male sexual aggression. The availability of abortion removes the one legitimized reason that women have had for refusing sex besides the headache." "Privacy v. Equality," reprinted in *Feminism Unmodified* (Cambridge: Harvard University Press, 1987), 93–102, 99. However, in later articles, she argues that legal abortion under the rubric of equality is a means of subverting male domination, as noted in the text.

24. MacKinnon, *Reflections*, 1324.

25. Reva Siegel, "Reasoning from the Body: A Historical Perspective on Abortion Regulation and Questions of Equal Protection," *Stanford Law Review* (1992): 261–381, 267.

26. Ruth Colker, "An Equal Protection Analysis of United States Reproductive Health Policy: Gender, Race, Age, and Class," *Duke Law Journal* (1991): 324–64, 329.

27. Mortality rates from illegal and unsafe abortion worldwide prompted the 1995 United Nations conferences in Cairo and Beijing to adopt a clause endorsing acceptance of the procedure in the name of (population control and) women's health.

28. It should be noted that some illegal pregnancy termination services were remarkably safe. The most well-known safe illegal abortion underground clinic was known simply as "Jane," though many "Janes" were involved. It arranged and performed over eleven thousand procedures in the Chicago area between 1969 and 1973 without a fatality. Lindsy Van Gelder, "The Jane Collective: Seizing Control," *Ms.* (September/October 1991): 83–85.

29. This information was provided by the Reproductive Rights Alliance, P.O. Box 788, Johannesburg, South Africa 2000, where I spent several months in 1996 working with and learning from Michelle O'Sullivan, Loveday Penn-Kekana, Fezeka Baliso, Joanne Fedler, and Cathi Albertyn.

30. United Nations, "Abortion Policies: A Global Review," vol. 3 (1995).

31. Jane Perlez, "Romania's Communist Legacy: Abortion Culture," *New York Times*, 21 November 1996, A3.

32. Loretta Ross, "A Simple Human Right," *On the Issues*, vol. 3, no. 2 (Spring 1992).

33. Connie Chan, "Reproductive Issues Are Essential Survival Issues for the

Asian American Communities," in *From Abortion to Reproductive Freedom*, Marlene Gerber Fried, ed. (Boston: South End Press, 1990), 175–78.

34. Statements concerning the mortality rates of childbirth can be found in nearly every women's health journal and publication. Specifically, see Gordon and books and articles written by Ann Oakley (some are cited in the bibliography). See also Emily Martin, *The Woman in the Body* (Boston: Beacon Press, 1987).

35. "Early screening for ectopic pregnancy in high-risk women avoids emergency surgery and allows for elective, conservative treatment, a study has shown." This was the caption in the second quarter *Family Planning Association* bulletin in 1994. The report was originally published in Cacciatore et al., *The Lancet* 343, (1994): 517–18.

36. Some feminists view access to technology as the extension of the right to life. Because denial of these services threatens women's health and survival, our right to life is violated. For example, see Lynda Barry, "Right to Life," *Ms.* (May/June 1995): 96 ("I knew I had to make a choice. And I knew I had to choose life. *My* life.").

37. Cornell, 21.

38. Alison Jaggar, "Sexual Difference and Sexual Equality," in *Theoretical Perspectives on Sexual Difference*, Deborah Rhode, ed. (New Haven: Yale University Press, 1990): 239–56, 251–52.

39. Marilyn Frye, "The Possibility of Feminist Theory," in *Theoretical Perspectives on Sexual Difference*, Deborah Rhode, ed. (New Haven: Yale University Press, 1990): 174–84, 180.

40. Cornell, 232.

41. Sylvia Law, "Rethinking Sex and the Constitution," *University of Pennsylvania Law Review* (1984): 955–1040. Law is widely regarded as a leading advocate in the usage of the equality doctrine to preserve access to abortion. She is cited in Garrow's *Liberty and Sexuality* as one of the premier promoters of this approach (pages 614 and 629). Justice Ruth Bader Ginsburg is the other person credited with advocacy of the Equal Protection Clause as applicable to abortion. I consider her insightful remarks on this approach toward the end of this chapter.

42. Law, 955.

43. Law, 969.

44. Law, 1007.

45. Olsen, *Unraveling Compromise*; MacKinnon, *Reflections*; Jed Rubenfeld, "The Right of Privacy," *Harvard Law Review* (1989): 737–807. Also, many briefs have since employed an equal-protection framework. For example, see selected amicus briefs submitted in *Webster v. Reproductive Health Services*, reprinted in the special double issue of the *Women's Rights Law Reporter* (Fall/Winter 1989).

46. Gerald Gunther, *Constitutional Law*, 12th ed. (New York: Foundation Press, 1991), 656.

47. I include an excerpt from this case:

Man is, or should be, woman's protector and defender. The natural and proper timidity and delicacy which belongs to the female evidently unfits it for many of the occupations of civil life. The constitution of the family organization, which is founded in divine ordinance, as well as in the nature of things, indicates the domestic sphere as that which properly belongs to the domain and functions of womanhood. [The] paramount destiny and mission of woman are to fulfill the noble and benign offices of wife and mother. This is the law of the Creator.

Gunther notes that Justice Brennan cites this *Bradwell* concurrence as evidence of the traditional paternalistic attitude of the bench. Gunther, 959, fn. 1.

48. See *Reed v. Reed*, 404 U.S. 71 (1971); *Frontiero v. Richardson*, 411 U.S. 677 (1973).

49. *Craig v. Boren*, 428 U.S. 190 (1976) (striking down Oklahoma statute that prohibited the sale of alcohol to males under 21 and females under 18). Reaffirmed in *Mississippi Univ. for Women v. Hogan*, 458 U.S. 718 (1982) (striking down women-only policy of School of Nursing).

50. *United States v. Virginia*, 522 U.S. 2264, 2274 (1996).

51. 522 U.S. at 2288 (Rehnquist, C.J., concurring).

52. 522 U.S. at 2306 (Scalia, J., dissenting).

53. Colker, 87.

54. Colker, 87.

55. Colker, 87.

56. J. Ralph Lindgren, "Rethinking the Grounds for Reproductive Freedom," in *Women's Rights and the Rights of Man*, A-J. Arnaud and Elizabeth Kingdom, eds. (Aberdeen, Scotland: Aberdeen University Press, 1990), 109–15, 114.

57. Colker, 104.

58. *Geduldig v. Aiello*, 417 U.S. 484 (1974) (state's decision to exclude pregnancy from coverage under disability insurance is not sex-based discrimination as required for a violation of the Equal Protection Clause). But see Justice Brennan's dissent, joined by Justices Douglas and Marshall: "By singling out for less favorable treatment a gender-linked disability peculiar to women, the State has created a double standard for disability compensation . . . dissimilar treatment of men and women, on the basis of physical characteristics inextricably limited to one sex, inevitably constitutes sex discrimination." 417 U.S. at 501. See also *Cleveland Bd. of Educ. v. LaFleur*, 414 U.S. 632 (1974) (involving mandatory maternity leave policy for pregnant school teachers).

59. MacKinnon, *Reflections*, 1322.

60. It reads: "This subsection shall not require employer to pay health insurance benefits for abortion, except where the life of the mother would be endangered if

the fetus were carried to term, or except where medical complications have arisen from abortion."

61. Siegel argues, "Only in *Thornburgh v. American College of Obstetricians and Gynecologists*, some thirteen years after *Roe*, did the Court begin to address the constitutional question in terms that broke sufficiently with *Roe*'s physiological framework to situate the abortion decision and its regulation within a larger social context," in "Reasoning from the Body," *Stanford Law Review* 44 (1992), 261–381, 349.

62. 112 S. Ct. at 2809.

63. *Personnel Administrator of Mass. v. Feeney*, 442 U.S. 256 (1979).

64. Colker, 84.

65. Colker, *An Equal Protection Analysis of Reproductive Health*, 360.

66. Siegel, 367.

67. Ruth Bader Ginsburg, William T. Joyner Lecture on Constitutional Law, "Some Thoughts on Autonomy and Equality in Relation to *Roe v. Wade*," Address before the University of North Carolina School of Law, 6 April 1984, reprinted in *North Carolina Law Review* (1985): 375–86.

68. Madison Lecture, cited in Senate Report, 103d Cong., 30 June 1993, 1–49, 18.

69. Confirmation Hearings, Senate Transcript Report, 103rd Congress, 30 June 1993.

70. Senate Report, 19.

71. Anita Allen, "The Proposed Equal Protection Fix for Abortion Law: Reflections on Citizenship, Gender, and the Constitution," *Harvard Journal of Law and Public Policy* (1995): 419–55, 421.

72. Allen, 421.

73. The Equal Protection Clause is only one potential means of advocating an equality perspective. Perhaps American feminists should consider advocacy of a Charter of Rights and Freedoms, as exists in Canada (see, *R v. Morgantaler*, 44 DLR 385, 1 SCR 30 [1988]) or rejuvenating the struggle for an Equal Rights Amendment.

74. Petchesky, 388.

75. Petchesky, 85.

76. Furthermore, male sterility can be concealed if therapeutic donor insemination is utilized. However, if a woman is infertile, this fact becomes evident if a child is beget by alternative means, because she will not appear pregnant. Some infertile women wear a prosthetic womb during the months before adoption to simulate pregnancy.

77. Maureen Freely, "Left Holding the Baby," *The Guardian* (January 1995): 4–5.

78. It should be noted that a few feminist theorists have bridged this gap, lamenting the institution of motherhood while celebrating mothers. Maureen Freely cites Anne Oakley in England and Adrienne Rich (as well as Barbara Katz Rothman) in the United States. See the bibliography for reference details.

79. Another interesting example of the polarization of motherhood involves entertainer and social-gadfly Madonna. The public was shocked to learn of Madonna's desire to become a mother, as if pregnancy and motherhood are things an independent "material girl" wouldn't want: too suburban, too soccer-mom-ish. Again, the public is guilty of subscribing to these polarized views of motherhood as inherently conservative and non-motherhood as more feminist, unless the pregnant woman is a teenager or a woman of color. (Racist and ageist prejudice is also a part of the political right's polarization of motherhood.)

80. Michelle Stanworth, "The Deconstruction of Motherhood," in *Reproductive Technologies: Gender, Motherhood, and Medicine*, Michelle Stanworth, ed. (Cambridge: Polity Press, 1987), 1–35, 35. See also Barbara Berg, "Listening to the Voices of the Infertile," in *Reproduction, Ethics and the Law*, Joan Callahan, ed. (Bloomington: Indiana University Press, 1995), 80–108 ("Let us make sure that when we make a stand against the pronatalist motherhood mandate, we do not oppose mothering.") 85.

81. Fried and Ross, 1.

82. Janet Callum, Rebecca Chalker, Janice Raymond, Robyn Rowland, "RU 486: Yes & No," *Ms.* (March/April 1993): 33–37.

7

FINAL THOUGHTS

his book presents arguments for a comprehensive assessment of technological intervention in the womb that relies upon a praxis feminist methodology and a materialist feminist explanation of sex-equality. It is my goal to outline a home language within which a good-faith dialogue about the substance of reactions to particular technologies can occur. In addition to outlining the theoretical foundations of this paradigm, it is useful to briefly sketch my intuitions regarding the substance of what a materialist feminist response to technological intervention in the womb might include.

Some Intuitions

In 1989 Christine Overall edited a book (largely by Canadian women) that included essays on birth control, assisted conception, prenatal technology, and birth. Not only is this compilation technologically comprehensive, but one of the essays considers feminist principles for assessing all technological intervention in the womb. Margrit Eichler's intention was to describe some minimal principles that should be used with reference to all technologies. She outlined eight policy suggestions:

1. Each reproductive technology needs to be evaluated separately with respect to its overall social desirability.
2. In choosing a particular technology, in all instances the safest, least invasive, simplest technique available should be employed before others are tried.
3. Any woman or man has the sole right to accept or refuse all treatments affecting his or her reproductive processes.

4. Stringent criteria as to what constitutes informed consent/decision making must be developed and enforced.

5. Legislation should prohibit individuals and organizations from arranging, for their own profit, transactions involving genetic materials and reproductive processes, and provide penalties for those who do.

6. Semen, eggs, and embryos can be used only with explicit informed consent of the donors.

7. National standards must be set for compulsory short-term and long-term follow-up of all reproductive technologies.

8. Everybody has the right to an environment free of agents that create and contribute to infertility.[1]

This list is extremely constructive. Of course, if we place it within the theoretical context of materialist feminism, it must also include guidelines for reforming the social institutions that situate women and technology, like education, law, and the family. Certainly any materialist feminist agenda would address the inadequacies—and, perhaps, domination—present in these social structures. A few amendments and additions to Eichler's list follow.

1. Add, "9. All women should be accorded the same access to reproductive health care options."

The phrase "all women" refers to universal coverage of reproductive health care. Once the effect of the good itself is esteemed because it fosters the self-determination of women, access and feasibility for all women are integral facets of the anti-subordination perspective.

> Reproductive technology is a *positive social need* of all women of childbearing age, not a necessary evil or a matter of private choice. It is a positive benefit that society has an obligation to provide to all who seek it, just as it provides education and health benefits.[2]

The social stratification condoned, indeed promulgated, by those urging state neutrality under the right to privacy should be avoided here because materialist feminism is acutely concerned with protecting the most subordinated elements of society. Lesbian, young, poor, and other women forgotten by the right to privacy are the constituency of primary concern to praxis feminists. Not only is demographic diversity remembered (indeed, heralded) but women of various health status should be covered under the rubric of materialist feminism. Women at different stages of childbearing should be treated and psychological testing requirements rejected under a materialist feminist framework. Further, women's autonomy should be safeguarded regardless of fetal development because the fetus is an entity developing *within the medium of a woman's body.* Regardless of a woman's particular condition, pregnant or not, most women value their own health and well-being. It is not in the interests of anyone, male or female, to self-inflict bodily harm. When a woman chooses abortion or water birth or IVF, we should assume that she has considered the impact and weighed her situation in the context of her own life. Pregnant women should not be deemed impaired citizens in need of supercilious "supervision" by the state or doctors or partners. Intervening in women's lives in order to (possibly) sustain fetal life seems to be more of an indication of society's condescending attitude toward women, especially poor minority women,[3] rather than an indication of a true pro-life mentality. Consequently, regardless of age, class, sexuality, and physical state, all women must have free informed choice among the options we deem appropriate as a prerequisite for equality.

    2. Add, "10. All approved reproductive health care options and services should be free."

What is meant by "free"? This word has double meaning. On one hand it is a monetary notion. No reproductive arrangements should involve the exchange of money. Like organ donation more generally, the use of sperm, eggs, and reproductive organs should not be a profit-making or fee-generating enterprise, avoiding commercialization and commodification of the body (as implied by number 5). Reproductive technology should be available and administered with public funds like food stamps and subsidized housing because reproductive health and control are integral to the survival of individual women and the social status of women as a group.

The other meaning assigned to the term "free" refers to free will: all donors and participants should be required to give explicit consent (supplementing number 6). This means that procedures such as sterilization, court-mandated Cesarean sections, fetal corrective surgery, and laparoscopic egg recovery require the explicit consent of the individual patient. Consequently, post mortem ventilation (PMV) is deemed unjust because the woman's body is being used without her express authorization, unless a living will exists that states otherwise. (PMV should become one of the routine questions on all organ-donation forms.)

3. Amend number 4 to say "fully" informed.

Having stated that all technological intervention must be free, it is important to clarify the conditions for free will. All patients should be fully informed. This means that free counseling that is discussion-oriented (rather than instructive) be made available (though not mandated). A woman should fully understand the nature and quality of any proposed invasion of her person prior to its occurrence. Like a hairdresser who has a special skill, the doctor offers a service and the recipient retains control of whether it will be administered. Women should be encouraged to scrutinize and select doctors and practitioners carefully, rather than accept cruel, disrespectful, or inadequate care.[4]

There are two exceptions to the informed-consent model to consider. First, emergency situations pose an exception to the requirement of free and informed consent prior to intervention. American tort law commonly ascribes a three-part rule to the "emergency principle": (1) the patient must be unconscious or without the capacity to consent, (2) time must be of the essence, and (3) a reasonable person would consent under the circumstances.[5] However, the patient and doctor(s) should establish ahead of time (in a cool moment) what might constitute an emergency so that this emergency principle does not grant unmitigated power to doctors.

Second, discussions of free and informed choice inevitably concern the difficulty of determining when exactly a person becomes informed and free enough to meet this nebulous standard. An entire literature is dedicated to exploring this large and complicated set of ethical and social theoretical questions—especially in a day and age of managed health care plans where choosing a doctor is somewhat restricted. However, I do recommend that counseling be in the patient's first language and in terms that are comprehensible. Public schools should educate all children about reproduction and sexuality, and a national table of the success rates, risks, and safety of all FDA-approved technologies should be published annually and made available to every citizen. These simple steps will help eliminate the coercion, extreme duress, and mistaken understanding that often characterize doctor-patient relationships.

4. Amend number 4 to read "choice" instead of "consent."

Reproductive destiny should be about choice, not consent. It has already been noted that rather than the doctor telling and the patient acquiescing, patients should be given responsibility for their own treatment options. In addition to reforming how procedural decisions are made, attention should be paid to the choices themselves. To this end, companies and regulatory agencies should be encouraged to develop more "user controlled" technologies— methods that do not require regular contact with a health professional. In comparison with the "free choice" advocated by privacy feminists, true choice requires certain governmental regulations and assurances with respect to quality of choice and provision.

At present, standards for research, experimentation, and development are monitored by different agencies and commissions on various national and local levels, the FDA possessing the greatest amount of influence. Carl Djerassi's exploration of the critical issues surrounding the allocation and social acceptance of the birth-control pill in the United States suggests that the FDA is a highly inefficient and inappropriate agency for monitoring and approving reproductive technologies.[6] Further, an article by Janet Benshoof, president of the Center for Reproductive Law and Policy, claims that the FDA is not an objective information warehouse, but a politically charged entity. She argues that the FDA failed to do its job by allowing six contraception companies to omit information regarding the morning-after capabilities of their products.

> There is a government agency designed to make sure companies give us full information: the FDA. But in this case, the FDA has kept quiet—despite the fact that, in my view, the current omission clearly violates the Food, Drug and Cosmetic Act,

which forbids "misleading" drug labeling, and the agency's own regulations for oral contraceptives, which require makers to list all of a product's risks and *benefits*.[7]

Benshoof filed a petition succcessfully arguing that the six contraceptives were misbranded.[8] Can the FDA be trusted to approve, and deny women access to, technologies that may affect not only their health, but also their social status?

Regulation and safety measures necessarily promote true choice because choice depends upon the existence of qualitative options to select. Individual nations, or perhaps nation states or counties, should be encouraged, if not required, to establish their own "tables" correlating clinic success rates with infertility treatments, Cesarean rates, standard procedures, typical waiting periods, and so on.[9] For example, the Fertility and Clinic Success Rate and Certification Act of 1992 (originally sponsored by Congressman Ron Wyden) requires programs to report success rates for various assisted conception technologies to the Center for Disease Control (CDC). However, this has yet to be implemented due to funding difficulties.

In addition to improving drug and device approval, medical education should be reformed such that doctors are better able—both as counselors and health providers—to facilitate choice. The Accreditation Council for Graduate Medical Education (ACGME) sets minimum standards for what doctors should be taught. So that doctors are truly service providers and not political agents, the ACGME should require that all prospective obstetrician gynecologists be trained in abortion, for example.[10]

Of course, these intuitions (dreams?) are highly controversial and could each be the subject of a book in their own right. Indeed, much further explication and research regarding mechanisms for ensuring informed choice and quality of options should be researched, explicated, and debated by experts in these particular fields. Having outlined the theoretical language within which I encourage this debate to occur, I merely wanted to suggest some substantive possibilities.

To summarize, rather than requiring XX behavior of all women, a more appropriate response to reproductive technology focuses on government action. A realistic assessment of both technology and women suggests that reproductive technology can be women-friendly under certain conditions levied by the state. Confronting gender inequality and the diverse experiences and preferences of women requires serious state activism.

> [W]e cannot be free [and equal] unless we are provided with certain positive resources which allow us to develop ourselves and exercise freedom effectively. . . . the idea of the welfare state is that certain needs and interests of citizens in a society are of such fundamental importance that society itself must guarantee their fulfillment.[11]

Thus, my materialist feminist intuitions understand the welfare state as being precisely about social justice because who we are is a function of social context, community, and culture.[12] Because gender directly dictates social standing, expectation, and limitation, needs and fulfillment of needs should be relative to these particular inequalities. This context-aware view of gender asks that the state redistribute at a certain material level such that equal opportunity is not only a theoretical possibility, but a social reality.[13] Instead of making unfair requests on, and assumptions about, women, the materialist feminist should ask the state to intervene and redistribute resources in an effort to confront gender discrimination. In arguing this same point, Rhonda Copelon writes, "To treat a woman's poverty and her inability to exercise choice as a consequence of personal failure, rather than of public policy and the market conditions it produces, is a dangerous fiction."[14] If the unequal distribution of resources and natural characteristics prejudice certain people to have greater autonomy than others, then any society claiming to value justice and equality has a duty to redistribute such conditions of self-realization.

> [The potential for autonomy] can not be instituted in a class-divided society with widespread economic and political inequality and deep conflicts of interest. . . . if autonomy is a vital interest, and if vital interests of each person are to count equally (as the Kantian principle of respect for all people requires), then equal weight should be given to the promotion of all citizens' autonomy.[15]

155

Therefore, I advocate a truly socialist response to reproductive technology. This praxis feminist materialist approach mirrors the socialists' intent: "setting people free from the condition of material dependence that has imprisoned them since the beginning of time."[16] Praxis feminism places the realities of sex within the scope of social justice more generally because public education, subsidized housing, and welfare benefits condition women's choices about, and the implications of, sexual reproduction. Broad social change and substantive equality are intimate elements of the praxis feminist vision, a truly intersectionist framework. Consequently, in endorsing a particular kind of feminism, I implicitly honor a specific approach to justice and the state.

In endorsing materialist feminism as the most praxis feminist response to technological intervention in the womb, a holistic category, I implicitly commit myself to a certain approach to feminism and social change beyond the scope of technological intervention in the womb. Although I have limited myself to this arena, many of my comments regarding the strengths and weaknesses of various feminist paradigms are applicable to feminist advocacy in other contexts. I implicitly celebrate two aspects of feminism more generally, both of which deserve attention.

Law as a Mechanism of Social Change?

Advocacy of the Equal Protection Clause as a response to technological intervention in the womb represents not only a particular brand of materialist feminism, but a particular approach to the law. Specifically, I endorse the use of law as a means of social change. Is this defensible?

Consider these three brief criticisms of the law as a mechanism for social change. First, our legal institutions have always reinforced—if not created—serious gender inequalities. When the Constitution was drafted over two hundred years ago and our legal institutions were created, women were not considered citizens, and African-Americans were counted as three-fifths of a person.[17] Today, the nine-person Supreme Court boasts only two women, and the 1996-elected House of Representatives has a mere forty-nine women (11 percent) while the Senate contains only nine![18]

Second, the American Bar Association estimates that there are fifty lawyers in the 1996 Senate, and the House is composed of more than 40 percent lawyers.[19] Moreover, the number of lawyers involved in local politics and litigation that has impact on public policy is inestimable. Regardless of their particular ideology or party affiliation, almost all lawyers went to law school. Indeed, as the institutions that school the millions of lawyers who shape policy, law schools are powerful establishments. Although not every law school class is inspired by the Kingsfield-Socratic method, several articles and books have testified to the gender bias in law schools.[20] There are the individual stories of gross anti-women behavior such as the *Harvard Law Review*-produced parody in 1992 that included ridicule of recently deceased woman law professor Mary Jo Frug on the first anniversary of her fatal stabbing.[21] Although 40 percent of law degrees awarded in 1989 went to women, law reviews and law faculty remain overwhelmingly male-populated.[22] The lack of women of color faculty at Harvard University Law School compelled Professor Derrick Bell to do more than chastise his employer's hiring practices; he filed a complaint with the U.S. Department of Education's Office of Civil Rights and he left, seeking refuge at New York University School of Law.[23]

Third, the law itself is no codification of feminist ideas. It is only in this century that the Constitution was amended to allow women to vote. Many of the current rules of evidence turn myths about women's sexuality into legal norms.[24] Also, legal discourse is unable to capture the social differences between men and women. For example, the "reasonable man standard" is a common element of judicial decisions. Judges ask, "Did x act reasonably in making y decision or doing z action?" Perhaps it would be more accurate to refer to this inquiry as the reasonable bourgeois-white-man standard. Similarly, Lynne Henderson argues that the law is incapable of recognizing the phenomena of empathy, which she defines as:

(1) feeling the emotion of another; (2) understanding the experience of another, both effectively and cognitively, often achieved by imagining oneself to be in the position of the other; and (3) action brought about by experiencing the distress of another (hence the confusion of empathy with sympa-

thy and compassion). The first are ways of knowing, the third forms a catalyst for action.[25]

Simply, the institutions that make our laws, the institutions that shape our lawyers, and the law itself have never been particularly woman-friendly enclaves. Can feminists use the law to effect social change in the twenty-first century? Is it naive to advocate a seemingly largely legal response to technological intervention in the womb? Moreover, if legal institutions and the law itself are part of the social structure that shapes gender inequality, is it self-defeating to advocate use of the legal system?

Feminists should "take back the law as a tool for social justice by remaking the institutions [and codes] of power, beginning with their intellectual foundation in the law schools."[26] We should continue to publish studies about women's experiences in law schools, demand affirmative-action policies for law reviews, and lobby hiring committees to hire more women, particularly women of color. In the activist tradition of our pioneer mothers—Elizabeth Cady Stanton, Emma Goldman, Barbara Jordan, Ruth Bader Ginsburg, and others—some of us should enter these dark chambers and turn on the lights! At a recent Northwestern University Symposium titled, "Can Feminists use the Law to Effect Social Change in the 1990s?" all four participants agreed that "while law can still be an instrument for change, the first order of business for feminists in the 1990s is to change law itself—not merely its doctrines and outcomes, but also legal institutions and lawyers' professional identity, as well as epistemological and metaphysical underpinnings of accepted modes of legal reasoning."[27] We should not become part of the dominant canon, but rather infiltrate it, like termites eating away at the foundations of a big white house until the happy patrons realize that serious remodeling is necessary.

This renovation requires feminist contribution within the system as well as outside it. "Political and moral commitment on the part of activists and scholars is necessary for the successful creation of a feminist jurisprudence that finally puts women into the Constitution on female rather than male terms."[28] Consequently, although I advocate using the law as a mechanism of social change, I am not insensitive to the serious obstacles that must not simply be hurdled, but eliminated altogether.

Second, even a reformed legal system is no messiah. Even if we successfully re-create the law and the institutions that shape the law in our own image, they are what we might call "public"—systems that shape and affect all the people in a given community. However, inequalities exist in our personal lives too. "Feminism must reach far beyond the scope of law and what has been traditionally thought of as public life."[29] We must always remember that the personal is political.

It is exactly because of my sensitivity to the limits of the law that I endorse the equality perspective; it transcends the public/private dichotomy. While the language of a "right to privacy" reinforces the idea of a separate space, a place where we are free of government interference, advocacy of equal respect and concern can be broadly applied. Equality is something we are, something we experience, something we feel in our interpersonal relationships and "private" decisions as well as our public life. Consequently, although equality may have a legal foundation and connotation, it can be utilized as a broad political vision.[30]

Thus, although the materialist feminism I endorse seems highly legal—and, as a political institution, the law is complicitous in the shaping of our gender inequality—we can and should rescue this powerful weapon and wield it in the name of gender justice beyond the confines of American public law but also in our personal lives under the broad rubric of equality.

Feminism as Feminisms

I believe that there is a plethora of ideas and authors united by a core feminism, a common constituency and common mission: to identify the cause(s) of oppression/inequality of women and suggest sources and mechanisms of effecting change in the name of justice. We may disagree about sources of oppression and plans of action, but it is important that we remember and even celebrate our commonality as feminists. If we are prepared to listen, we can learn from each other. Ruth Colker calls this a good-faith dialogue. As Elizabeth Gross contends:

> Feminist theory seeks a new discursive space, a space where women can write, read, and think as women. This space will

encourage a proliferation of voices, instead of hierarchy struc-
turing them, a plurality of perspectives and interests instead of
the monopoly of one—new kinds of questions and different
kinds of answers. No one form would be privileged as the truth,
the correct interpretation, the right method: rather, knowledges, methods, interpretations can be judges and used according to their appropriateness to give a context, a specific
strategy and particular effects.[31]

In these pages I have tried to honor the wide variety that characterizes feminist theory, from radical constructions of sex as the significant fact of being, to no recognition of sex at all. Describing this
rainbow of feminisms, Rosemarie Tong writes:

[I] take vicarious pleasure and pride in the different thoughts
women have conceived in order to liberate themselves from
oppression. To be sure, some of these thoughts have sent
women stumbling down cul-de-sacs; but most of them have
brought women at least a few steps closer to liberation. Because
feminist thought is a kaleidoscope, the reader's preliminary im-
pression may be one of chaos and confusion, of dissension and
disagreement, of fragmentation and splintering. . . . Appar-
ently, not the truth but truths are setting women free.[32]

Having venerated the importance of this good-faith dialogue, I
clearly endorse one type of feminism over the others: praxis.

To praxis feminism, difference among women doesn't just matter,
it is undeniable. Rather than formulating a conception of "woman"
and then explaining how it "covers" the black lesbian advertising
executive in Chicago, the Irish heterosexual law student in Boston,
and the sixteen year old Chinese domestic worker in Smallville,
praxis feminism begins with our diversity and creates a theory that
both encompasses and understands it.

Praxis feminism is realistic as it does not apologize for, celebrate,
or ignore both sex and gender, but confronts them both—as separate, yet connected, facts of being. Moreover, praxis feminism takes
women as we are currently situated—in trailer parks, public housing
units, and four-bedroom, five-and-a-half-bath Victorian homes, as
WASP, black, and Chicana. This realism bolsters the viability of its

prescriptions for justice; because it is socially honest, hopeful, fully inclusive of women, practical, and so on, it has a better chance of success.

Although I have endorsed materialist feminism as the most praxis-oriented, I maintain that the other feminisms presented here are indeed feminisms because they contain the core requisites. Critical feminist writing does not need to be rejectionist. It should be constructive and have a purpose beyond selling books or gaining tenure. Remember Goldilocks. She found one bowl of porridge too hot and another bowl too cold before finding a third bowl just right—but she was always tasting porridge. So long as we are all concerned with identifying and rectifying the oppression of women, we are united in sisterhood.

Notes

1. Margrit Eichler, "Some Minimal Principles," in *The Future of Human Reproduction*, Christine Overall, ed. (Toronto: Women's Press, 1989), 226–37.

2. Petchesky, *Abortion and Woman's Choice*, 387.

3. "A recent survey found that court orders for Cesarean sections were sought against 15 women in 11 states. Of those 15 women, seven were black, five were Asian or African, and only three were white. Four of the fifteen did not speak English as their primary language." Colker, 151.

4. *Glamour* magazine included a list of "Ten Labor Questions You Should Ask Your Doctor" in the May 1995 issue encouraging women to take active roles in their health care. The list included: What is your Cesarean rate? Do you have experience using forceps and/or vacuum extractors? What is your episiotomy rate? What percentage of your patients' babies do you deliver yourself? How many of your patients are given epidurals? Pitocin? Other drugs? Routine IVs? Fetal monitoring? How many people can I have with me in the delivery room? How long will you be with me when I'm in labor? Can my partner stay with me during Cesarean? Can I have the birth videotaped? I believe that answers to these questions should be catalogued in "tables" made available to the public.

5. W. Page Keeton, *Prosser and Keeton on Torts*, 5th ed. (St. Paul, Minn.: West Publishing, 1984).

6. Carl Djerassi, *The Politics of Contraception* (San Francisco: W. H. Freeman, 1979), 79–87 and 221–25. Another example of inefficient approval of a contraceptive, specifically the cervical cap, was noted in a recent article by Rebecca Chalker, "A New (Old) Contraceptive Choice," *Ms.* (November/December 1992), 58–60.

7. Janet Benshoof, "Ever Had a Pregnancy Scare?" *Glamour* (May 1995): 121.

8. The FDA granted Benshoof's petition and approved the emergency contraceptives as safe and effective.

9. In 1995, The Human Fertilization and Embryology Authority in England decided to create "League Tables" for fertility clinics. Jeremy Laurence reported in *The Independent*, 29 January 1995, "Success rates for fertility clinics are to be published after pressure from patients' groups worried that some centers were concealing their figures."

10. In fact, ACGME tried to establish this as national policy, and Congress blocked this effort. On the history of the fight over ACGME regulations, see "Compromise on Abortion Training Reached," *Ob/Gyn News* (15 July 1996): 5.

11. Nicola Lacey, "Theories of Justice and the Welfare State," *Social and Legal Studies* (1992): 20–39, 25.

12. Lacey, 23, 37.

13. Lacey, 39.

14. Rhonda Copelon, "From Privacy to Autonomy: The Conditions for Sexual and Reproductive Freedom," in *From Abortion to Reproductive Freedom: Transforming a Movement*, Marlene Gerber Fried, ed. (Boston: South End Press, 1990), 27–44, 38.

15. Richard Lindley, *Autonomy* (London: Macmillan, 1986), 139.

16. Leon Baradat, *Political Ideologies*, 3rd ed. (New Jersey: Prentice Hall, 1978), 168.

17. For an extremely thorough discussion of the legacy of the Founding Fathers upon current constitutional trends, see Jennifer Nedelsky, *Private Property and the Limits of American Constitutionalism: The Madisonian Framework and its Legacy* (Chicago: University of Chicago Press, 1990) (especially chapter 6).

18. Also, a recent article by "Anne Tully," a pseudonym for a prosecutor in a large city district attorney's office, illustrates the difficult aspects of being a feminist in a notoriously socially conservative and sexist environment. Anne Tully [pseud.], "Working Inside the System," *On the Issues* (Winter 1997): 44–46.

19. For more information about lawyers in the government, contact the Government Affairs Office of the American Bar Association, 202–662–1764.

20. Lani Guinier, et al., "Becoming Gentlemen: Women's Experiences at One Ivy League Law School," *University of Pennsylvania Law Review* (1994): 1–100 (providing hard data regarding the oppressive experience of women in law school); Deborah Merrit and Barbara Reskin, "The Hidden Bias of Law Faculties," *Connecticut Law Tribune*, 21 September 1992; Peter Shane, "Why Are So Many People So Unhappy: Habits of Thought and Resistance to Diversity in Legal Education," *Iowa Law Review* (1990): 1033–56.

21. Linda Hirshman, "Sex and Money: Is Law School a Dead-End Street for Women?" *Northwestern University Law Review* (1993): 1265–72, 1266. See also the *New York Times* reporting of the incident: David Margolick, "At the Bar: In Attacking

the Work of a Slain Professor, Harvard's Elite Themselves Become a Target," *New York Times*, 17 April 1992, B16; Fox Butterfield, "Parody Puts Harvard Law Faculty in Sexism Battle," *New York Times*, 27 April 1992, A10.

22. See Guinier, *Becoming Gentlemen.*

23. In support of Bell's contention that women of color suffer systematic disadvantage in law school hiring, see Deborah Jones Merrit and Barbara Reskin, "The Hidden Bias of Law Faculties," *Connecticut Law Tribune*, 21 September 1992.

24. Joan Hoff, *Law, Gender, and Injustice: A Legal History of U.S. Women* (New York: New York University Press, 1991). Juliet Mitchell, "Women and Equality," in *Feminism and Equality*, Anne Phillips, ed. (New York: New York University Press, 1987), 24–43, 29 ("Bourgeois, capitalist law is a general law that ensures that everybody is equal before it: it is abstract and applies to all cases and all persons. . . . The law, then, enshrines the principles of freedom and equality—so long as you do not look at the particular unequal conditions of the people who are subjected to it."). Also see an editorial column in the *New York Times* following the hung jury in the Connecticut trial of Alex Kelly on rape charges where Lynn Hecht Schafran of the NOW Legal Defense and Education Fund discusses the Courts' repeated misunderstanding of evidence in rape cases. Lynn Hecht Schafran, "They Just Don't Get It about Rape," *New York Times*, 16 November 1996.

25. Lynne Henderson, "Legality and Empathy," in *Feminist Jurisprudence*, Patricia Smith, ed. (New York: Oxford University Press, 1993), 244–81, 246. See also Carol Rose, "Women and Property: Gaining and Losing Ground," *Virginia Law Review* (1992): 209–39.

26. Jane Larson, "Introduction: Can Feminists Use the Law to Effect Social Change in the 1990s?" Symposium at Northwestern University School of Law, reprinted in *Northwestern University Law Review* (1993): 1252–59.

27. Larson, 1254. For an excellent article on the potential to transform the law in our own image(s), see Patricia Williams, "Alchemical Notes: Reconstructing Ideals from Deconstructed Rights," *Harvard Civil Rights-Civil Liberties Law Review* (1987): 401–33 ("What is needed, therefore, is not the abandonment of rights language for all purposes, but an attempt to become multilingual in the semantics of each others'."). Williams, 410.

28. Hoff, 374.

29. Cornell, 27.

30. The equality approach is also capable of permeating the context of American legal discourse. Although my examination is largely limited to the United States, these technologies involve women everywhere. I believe it is more responsible to limit my focus nationally than to misrepresent other cultures and peoples by conflating contexts. Consequently, my legal and institutional references are very America-centric and I explore application of the various feminist frameworks mainly within the U. S. context. However, the equality perspective is the least

"American." To most other peoples, "privacy" refers to documents and records that the government and media cannot obtain without consent. Alternatively, the world's women can define the prerequisites for equality in their own social and political context. I am grateful to Michelle O'Sullivan of the Reproductive Rights Alliance, South Africa, for our many discussions regarding this point.

31. Elizabeth Gross, "What is Feminist Theory?" in *Feminist Challenges*, Elizabeth Gross and Carole Pateman, eds. (London: Allen and Unwin, 1986), 204.

32. Rosemarie Tong, *Feminist Thought: A Comprehensive Introduction* (San Francisco: Westview Press, 1989), 237–38.

Appendix A

State of the States: Gender Wage Gap

State of the States:
Gender Wage Gap

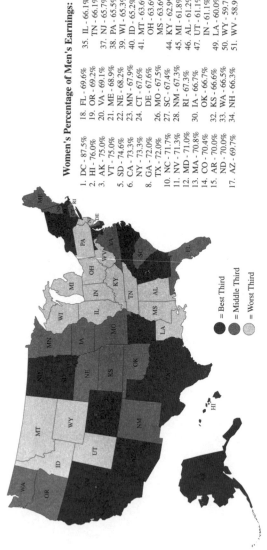

= Best Third

= Middle Third

= Worst Third

Women's Percentage of Men's Earnings:

1. DC - 87.5%	18. FL - 69.6%	35. IL - 66.1%
2. HI - 76.0%	19. OR - 69.2%	TN - 66.1%
3. AK - 75.0%	20. VA - 69.1%	37. NJ - 65.7%
VT - 75.0%	21. ME - 68.9%	38. PA - 65.5%
5. SD - 74.6%	22. NE - 68.2%	39. WI - 65.3%
6. CA - 73.3%	23. MN - 67.9%	40. ID - 65.2%
NY - 73.3%	24. CT - 67.6%	41. MT - 63.6%
8. GA - 72.0%	DE - 67.6%	OH - 63.6%
TX - 72.0%	26. MO - 67.5%	MS - 63.6%
10. NC - 71.7%	27. SC - 67.4%	44. KY - 62.9%
11. NV - 71.3%	28. NM - 67.3%	45. MI - 61.8%
12. MD - 71.0%	RI - 67.3%	46. AL - 61.2%
13. MA - 70.8%	30. IA - 66.7%	47. UT - 61.1%
14. CO - 70.4%	OK - 66.7%	IN - 61.1%
15. AR - 70.0%	32. KS - 66.6%	49. LA - 60.0%
ND - 70.0%	33. WA - 66.5%	50. WY - 59.7%
17. AZ - 69.7%	34. NH - 66.3%	51. WV - 58.9%

The ratio of median earnings of women working full-time, full-year to median earnings of men working full-time, full-year. IWPR analysis of 1990 Census data, Bureau of the Census, U.S. Department of Commerce. Copyright 1996 Institute for Women's Policy Research and the Center for Policy Alternatives.

For more information contact: The Center for Policy Alternatives at (202) 387-6030;
The Institute for Women's Policy Research at (202) 785-5100.

APPENDIX B

RESTRICTIONS ON MINORS' ACCESS TO ABORTION

State	One Parent	Two Parent	Content	Notice	Waiting Period	Mandatory Counseling	Judicial Bypass	Enforced/ Not Enforced	Enforced
AL	X		X				X		X
AK	X		X					X[1]	
AZ	X		X				X	X[1]	
AR		X		X	X		X		X
C A	X		X				X	X	
CO	X		X					X[1]	
CT						X			X
DE	X[2,5]			X	X		X		X
DC									
FL									
GA	X			X	X		X		X
HI									
ID		X		X	X				X
IL	X3			X	X		X	X[1]	
IN	X		X				X		X
IA	X[8]			X	X		X		X
KS	X			X		X	X		X
KY	X		X				X		X
LA	X		X				X		X
ME	X		X			X[4]	X		X

1. This statute has been declared unenforceable by a court or attorney general.
2. This statute also allows consent by or notice to a grandparent under certain circumstances.
3. This statute also allows consent of a grandparent.
4. This statute offers mandatory counseling as an alternative to one-parent or adult family member consent with a judicial bypass.
5. This requirement may be waived by a specified health professional under certain circumstances.
6. This statute also allows notice to a grandparent or adult sibling under certain circumstances.
7. This statute is a two-parent notice law interpreted as requiring notice to one parent.
8. This statute allows consent of or notice to a grandparent or certain other adult family members over the age of 25.

State	One Parent	Two Parent	Consent	Notice	Waiting Period	Mandatory Counseling	Judicial Bypass	Enjoined/ Not Enforced	Enforced
MD	X			X[5]					X
MA		X	X				X		X
MI	X		X				X		X
MN		X		X	X		X		X
MS		X	X				X		X
MO	X		X				X		X
MT	X			X	X		X	X[1]	
NE	X			X	X		X		X
NV	X			X			X	X[1]	
NH									
NJ									
NM	X		X					X[1]	
NY									
NC	X[2]		X				X		X
ND		X	X				X		X
OH	X[6]			X	X		X		X
OK									
OR									
PA	X		X				X		X
RI	X		X				X		X
SC	X[3]		X				X		X
SD	X			X	X			X[1]	
TN	X		X				X	X[1]	
TX									
UT	X[7]			X					X
VT									
VA									
WA									
WV	X			X[5]	X[5]		X		X
WI	X[8]		X				X		X
WY	X		X		X		X		X
TOTAL	32	6	22	16	13	3	31	10	29

Selected Bibliography

Allen, Anita. "The Proposed Equal Protection Fix for Abortion Law: Reflections on Citizenship, Gender, and the Constitution." *Harvard Journal of Law and Public Policy* (1995): 419–55.

Alpert, Jane. "Mother Right: A New Feminist Theory." *Ms.* (August 1973): 52–55, 88–94.

Andrews, Lori. *Between Strangers: Surrogate Mothers, Expectant Fathers, and Brave New Babies.* New York: Harper and Row, 1989.

———. "Surrogacy Wars." *California Lawyer* 12 (1992): 43–50.

Arch, Rebekah. "The Maternal-Fetal Rights Dilemma: Honoring a Woman's Choice of Medical Care during Pregnancy." *Journal of Contemporary Health Law and Policy* 12 (1996): 637–73.

Arendt, Hannah. *The Human Condition.* Chicago: University of Chicago Press, 1958.

Arditti, Rita, Renate D. Klein, and Shelley Minden, eds. *Test-Tube Women.* London: Pandora Press, 1984.

Babbington, Charles. "Abortion-Rights Group Broadens Focus." *The Washington Post,* 10 January 1993, A1.

Baehr, Ninia. *Abortion without Apology: A Radical History for the 1990s.* Boston: South End Press, 1990.

Baily, Margaret, J. Bradley Moritz, Robert B. Kelly, and Kathleen Marie Dixon. "A Case of Surrogate Pregnancy." *The Journal of Family Practice* 30 (1990): 19–26.

Balieu, Etienne Emile. *The Abortion Pill.* London: Century, 1991.

Barrett, Michéle. *Women's Oppression Today: The Marxist Feminist Encounter.* London: Verso, 1988.

Barry, Lynda. "Right to Life." *Ms.* (May/June 1995): 96.

Bartowski, Frances. *Feminist Utopias.* Lincoln: University of Nebraska Press, 1989.

Bartels, Dianne, Reinhard Priester, Dorothy Vawter, and Arthur Caplan, eds. *Beyond Baby M: Ethical Issues in New Reproductive Techniques.* Clifton, N.J.: Humana Press, 1990.

Basen, Gwynne, Margrit Eichler, and Abby Lippman, eds. *Misconceptions: The Social Construction of Choice and the New Reproductive and Genetic Technologies.* Hull, Quebec: Voyager Publishing, 1993 vol. 1, 1994 vol. 2.

Baur, Karla, and Robert Crooks. *Our Sexuality.* 4th ed. New York: Benjamin/Cummings, 1990.

Baxandall, Rosalyn. *Women and Abortion: The Body as Battleground.* Open Pamphlet Series. Westfield, N.J.: Open Media, 1992.

Benshoof, Janet. "Ever Had a Pregnancy Scare?" *Glamour* (May 1995): 121.

———. "Abortion Rights and Wrongs: Undue Burdens—The Rhetoric is Pro-Roe, but the reality is Anti-Choice." *The Nation* (14 October 1996): 19–20.

Benton, Elizabeth Carlin. "The Constitutionality of Pregnancy Clauses in Living Will Statutes." *Vanderbilt Law Review* 43 (1990): 1821–37.

Berer, Marge. "Breeding Conspiracies: Feminism and the New Reproductive Technologies." *Trouble and Strife* 9 (Summer 1986): 29–35.

Biale, Rachel. *Women and Jewish Law.* New York: Schocken Books, 1984.

Biehl, Janet. *Rethinking Ecofeminist Politics.* Boston: South End Press, 1991.

Birke, Lynda, Susan Himmelweit, and Gail Vines. *Tomorrow's Child: Reproductive Technology in the 90s.* London: Virago, 1990.

Bock, Gisela, and Susan James, eds. *Beyond Equality and Difference.* London: Routledge, 1992.

Brill, Alida. *Nobody's Business: The Paradoxes of Privacy.* Reading, Mass.: Addison-Wesley, 1990.

Burch, Timothy. "Incubator or Individual?" *Maryland Law Review* 54 (1995): 528–70.

Callahan, Joan. "Contraception or Incarceration: What's Wrong with This Picture?" *Stanford Law and Policy Review* 7 (Winter 1996): 67–77.

———, ed. *Reproduction, Ethics and the Law: Feminist Perspectives.* Bloomington: Indiana University Press, 1995.

Callum, Janet, and Rebecca Chalker. "RU 486: Yes & No." *Ms.* (March/April 1993): 33–37.

Chalker, Rebecca. "A New (Old) Contraceptive Choice." *Ms.* (November/December 1992): 58–60.

Chesler, Ellen. *Woman of Valor: Margaret Sanger and the Birth Control Movement in America.* New York: Simon and Schuster, 1992.

Childress, J. F.. "The Body as Property: Some Philosophical Reflections." *Transplantation Proceedings* 24 (October 1992): 2143–48.

Chodorow, Nancy. *The Reproduction of Mothering: Psychoanalysis and the Sociology of Gender.* Berkeley: University of California Press, 1978.

Cohen, Sherrill, and Nadine Taub, eds. *Reproductive Laws for the 1990s.* Clifton, N.J.: Humana Press, 1989.

Colker, Ruth. "An Equal Protection Analysis of United States Reproductive Health Policy: Gender, Race, Age, and Class." *Duke Law Journal* (1991): 324–64.

———. *Abortion & Dialogue.* Bloomington: Indiana University Press, 1992.

———. "The Practice of Theory." *Northwestern University Law Review* 87 (1993): 1273–85.

Congregation for the Doctrine of Faith. *Instruction on Respect for Human Life in Its Origins and on the Disunity of Procreation.* Released by the Vatican 10 March 1981.

Copelon, Rhonda. "From Privacy to Autonomy: The Conditions for Sexual and Reproductive Freedom." In *From Abortion to Reproductive Freedom: Transforming a Movement,* edited by Marlene Gerber Fried. Boston: South End Press, 1990.

———. "What's Missing from the Abortion Debate." *Ms.* (September/October 1992): 86–87.

Corea, Gena. *The Mother Machine.* London: Women's Press, 1985.

Corea, Gena, et al. *Man-Made Women: How New Reproductive Technologies Affect Women.* London: Hutchinson, 1985.

Cornell, Drucilla. *The Imaginary Domain.* New York: Routledge, 1995.

Coward, Rosalind. *Patriarchal Precedents: Sexuality and Social Relations.* London: Routledge, 1983.

Daly, Mary. *Gyn/Ecology: The Metaethics of Radical Feminism.* Boston: Beacon Press, 1978.

———. *Pure Lust: Elemental Feminist Philosphy.* Boston: Beacon Press, 1984.

de Beauvoir, Simone. *The Second Sex.* Harmondsworth: Penguin, 1953.

De Gama, Katherine. "A Brave New World? Rights Discourse and the Politics of Reproductive Autonomy." In *Feminist Theory and Legal Strategy,* edited by Anne Bottomley and Joanne Conaghan. Oxford: Blackwell, 1992.

de Lauretis, Teresa, ed. *Feminist Studies/Critical Studies.* Bloomington: Indiana University Press, 1986.

Derrida, Jacques. *Grammatologie.* Paris: Editions de Minout, 1967.

———. *Writing and Difference.* London: Routledge, 1978.

Diamond, Irene, and Gloria Orenstein, eds. *Reweaving the World: The Emergence of Ecofeminism.* San Francisco: Sierra Club Books, 1990.

Djerassi, Carl. *The Politics of Contraception.* San Francisco: W. H. Freeman, 1979.

Doane, Mary Anne. "Cyborgs, Origins and Subjectivity." In *Coming to Terms: Feminism, Theory, Politics,* edited by Elizabeth Weed. New York: Routledge, 1989.

Dworkin, Gerald. *The Theory and Practice of Autonomy.* Cambridge: Cambridge University Press, 1988.

Edwards, Robert, and Patrick Steptoe. *A Matter of Life: The Story of a Medical Breakthrough.* London: William Morrow and Co., 1980.

Eichler, Margrit, and Jeanne Lapointe. *On the Treatment of the Sexes in Research.* Ottawa: Social Sciences and Humanities Research Council of Canada, 1985.

Eisenstein, Zillah. *The Radical Future of Liberal Feminism.* Boston: Northeastern University Press, 1981.

———. *Feminism and Sexual Equality.* New York: Monthly Review Press, 1984.

Faludi, Susan. *Backlash: The Undeclared War Against American Women.* New York: Crown Publishers, 1991.

———. "I'm Not a Feminist, But I Play One on TV." *Ms.* (March/April 1995): 30–39.

Faux, Marian. *Crusaders: Voices from the Abortion Front.* New York: Carol Publishing, 1990.

Feminists for Life. *Mission Statement.* Issued in Washington D.C., 4 May 1994.

Findlen, Barbara, ed. *Listen Up: Voices from the Next Generation.* Seattle: Seal Press, 1995.

Fineman, Martha Albertson, and Isabel Karpin. *Mothers in Law: Feminist Theory and the Legal Regulation of Motherhood.* New York: Columbia University Press, 1995.

Firestone, Shulamith. *The Dialectic of Sex: The Case for a Feminist Revolution.* London: Women's Press, 1970.

Fox Keller, Evelyn. *Reflections on Gender and Science.* New Haven: Yale University Press, 1985.

Frazer, Elizabeth, and Nicola Lacey. *The Poltics of Community: A Feminist Critique of the Liberal-Communitarian Debate.* London: Harvester Wheatsheaf, 1993.

Freely, Maureen. "Left Holding the Baby." *The Guardian,* 23 January 1995, 4–5.

Fried, Marlene Gerber, ed. *From Abortion to Reproductive Freedom: Transforming a Movement.* Boston: South End Press, 1990.

Fried, Marlene Gerber, and Loretta Ross. *Reproductive Freedom: Our Right to Decide.* Open Pamphlet Series. Westfield, N.J.: Open Media, 1992.

Fuss, Diana. *Essentially Speaking: Feminism, Nature and Difference.* New York: Routledge, 1989.

Gallagher, Janet. "Prenatal Invasions and Interventions: Whats Wrong with Fetal Rights." *Harvard Women's Law Journal* 10 (1987): 9–58.

Garrow, David. *Liberty and Sexuality: The Right to Privacy and the Making of Roe vs. Wade.* New York: Macmillan, 1994.

Gilligan, Carol. *In a Different Voice.* Boston: Harvard University Press, 1982.

Ginsburg, Ruth Bader. "Some Thoughts on Autonomy and Equality in Relation to Roe v. Wade." *North Carolina Law Review* 63 (1985): 375–86.

———. "Sex Equality and the Constitution: The State of the Art." *Women's Rights Law Reporter* 14 (1992): 361–66.

Goggin, Malcolm, ed. *Understanding the New Politics of Abortion.* New York: Sage, 1993.

Gordon, Linda. *Woman's Body, Woman's Right: Birth Control in America.* New York: Penguin Books, 1977.

Greer, Germaine. *The Female Eunuch.* London: Harper Collins, 1970.

———. *The Madwoman's Underclothes.* New York: Atlantic Monthly Press, 1986.

Gostin, Larry, ed. *Surrogate Motherhood: Politics and Privacy.* Bloomington: Indiana University Press, 1990.

Griffin, Susan. *Woman and Nature: The Roaring Inside Her.* New York: Perennial Library, 1978.

———. "Split Culture." In *Healing the Wounds: The Promise of Ecofeminism,* edited by Judith Plant. Philadelphia: New Society Publishers, 1989.

Gross, Elizabeth. "Sexual Difference and the Problem of Essentialism." In *The Essential Difference*, edited by Naomi Schor and Elizabeth Weed. Bloomington: Indiana University Press, 1994.

Guinier, Lani, Michelle Fine, Jane Balin, Ann Bartow, and Deborah Lee Stachel. "Becoming Gentlemen: Women's Experiences at One Ivy League Law School." *University of Pennsylvania Law Review* 143 (1994): 1–100.

Haraway, Donna. *Simians, Cyborgs and Women.* New York: Routledge, 1991.

Harding, Sandra. *Whose Science? Whose Knowledge? Thinking from Women's Lives.* Ithaca: Cornell University Press, 1991.

Hirshman, Linda. "Sex and Money: Is Law School a Dead-End Street for Women?" *Northwestern University Law Review* 87 (1993): 1265–72.

Hoff, Joan. *Law, Gender, and Injustice: A Legal History of U.S. Women.* New York: New York University Press, 1991.

Holmes, Helen, Betty Hoskins, and Michael Gross, eds. *Birth Control and Controlling Birth: A Woman-Centered Analysis.* Clifton, N.J.: Humana Press, 1980.

———. *The Custom-Made Child? Women-Centered Perspectives.* Clifton, N.J.: Humana Press, 1981.

Holmes, Helen Bequaert, and Laura Purdy, eds. *Feminist Perspectives in Medical Ethics.* Bloomington: Indiana University Press, 1992.

Holmes, Helen Bequaert, ed. *Issues in Reproductive Technology.* New York: Garland Publishing, 1992.

hooks, bell. *Ain't I a Woman: Black Women and Feminism.* Boston: South End Press, 1981.

———. *Feminist Theory: From Margin to Center.* Boston: South End Press, 1984.

———. "A Feminist Challenge: Must We Call All Women Sister?" *Zeta* (February 1992): 19–22.

———. "Out of the Academy and Into the Streets." *Ms.* (July/August 1992): 80–82.

Horstmeyer, Eric. "Gestational Surrogacy." *University of Louisville Journal of Family Law* 32 (1994): 953–59.

Humm, Maggie, ed. *Modern Feminisms.* New York: Columbia University Press, 1992.

Hurst, Jane. "The History of Abortion in the Catholic Church: The Untold Story." Abortion in Good Faith Series. Washington, D.C.: Catholics for a Free Choice, 1989.

Irigaray, Luce. *Thinking the Difference for a Peaceful Revolution.* Translated by Karen Montin. London: Althone Press, 1994.

———. *The Irigaray Reader.* Edited by Maragret Whitford. Oxford: Blackwell Publishers, 1991.

Jaggar, Alison. "Political Philosophies of Women's Liberation." In *Feminism and Philosophy*, edited by Mary Vetterling-Braggin, Frederick Elliston, and Jane English. Totowa, N.J.: Rowman and Allanheld, 1977.

Jaggar, Alison, and Paula Rothenberg, eds. *Feminist Frameworks.* 3rd ed. New York: McGraw-Hill, 1993.

Johnsen, Dawn. "Shared Interests: Promoting Healthy Births without Sacrificing Women's Liberty." *Hastings Law Journal* 43 (1992): 569–614.

Jordan, James. "Incubating for the State: The Precarious Autonomy of Persistently Vegetative and Brain-Dead Pregnant Women." *Georgia Law Review* 22 (1988): 1103–65.

Kasindorf, Martin. "And Baby Makes Four," *Los Angeles Times Magazine* (20 January 1991): 10–16, 30–33.

Kingdom, Elizabeth. *What's Wrong with Rights?* Edinburgh: Edinburgh University Press, 1991.

Kirkup, Gill, and Laurie Smith Keller, eds. *Inventing Women: Science, Technology, and Gender.* Cambridge: Polity Press, 1992.

Kitzinger, Sheila. *Freedom and Choice in Childbirth.* London: Penguin Books, 1987.

Klass, Perri. "The Artificial Womb Is." *New York Times Magazine* (29 September 1996): 116–119.

Klein, Renate, ed. *Infertility: Women Speak Out about Their Experiences of Reproductive Medicine.* London: Pandora Press, 1989.

Kolbert, Kathryn, and David Gans. "Responding to *Planned Parenthood vs. Casey*: Establishing Neutrality Principles in State Constitutional Law." *Temple Law Review* 66 (Winter 1993): 1151–70.

Kozolanka, Kirsten. "Giving Up: The Choice that Isn't." In *Infertility: Women Speak Out,* edited by Renate D. Klein. London: Pandora Press, 1989.

Kuhn, Thomas. *The Structure of Scientific Revolutions.* Chicago: University of Chicago Press, 1962.

Lacey, Nicola. "Theories of Justice and the Welfare State." *Social and Legal Studies* (1992): 20–39.

Lader, Lawrence. *RU486: The Pill That Could End the Abortion Wars and Why American Women Don't Have It.* Reading, Penn.: Addison-Wesley, 1991.

Larson, Jane. "Introduction: Can Feminists Use the Law to Effect Social Change in the 1990s?" *Northwestern University Law Review* 87 (1993): 1252–59.

Lauritzen, Paul. "What Price Parenthood?" *Hastings Center Report* (March/April 1990): 38–46.

Law, Sylvia. "Rethinking Sex and the Constitution." *University of Pennsylvania Law Review* 132 (1984): 955–1040.

———. "Access to Reproductive Drugs and Devices." Prepared for the Bellagio Conference, 1996. On file with author.

Lindgren, J. Ralph. "Rethinking the Grounds for Reproductive Freedom." In *Women's Rights and the Rights of Man,* edited by A-J Arnaud and Elizabeth Kingdom. Aberdeen, Scotland: Aberdeen University Press, 1990, 109–16.

Liu, Athena. *Artifical Reproduction and Reproductive Rights.* Hong Kong: Dartmouth Publishing, 1991.

Lockard, Duane, and Walter F. Murphy. *Basic Cases in Constitutional Law.* 2nd ed. Washington, D.C.: Congressional Quarterly Press, 1987.

Longino, Helen. *Science as Knowledge: Values and Objectivity in Scientific Inquiry.* Princeton: Princeton University Press, 1990.

Lorde, Audre. "An Open Letter to Mary Daly." In *This Bridge Called My Back: Writings by Radical Women of Color,* edited by Cherrie Moraga and Gloria Anzaldua. New York: Kitchen Table, 1983.

————. *Sister Outsider: Essays and Speeches.* Trumansburg: Crossing Press, 1984.

Luker, Kristin. *Abortion and The Politics of Motherhood.* Berkeley: University of California Press, 1984.

MacKinnon, Catharine. "Feminism, Marxism, Method and the State: An Agenda for Theory." In *Feminist Theory: A Critique of Ideology,* edited by N. O. Keohane. Brighton: Harvester, 1982.

————. *Feminism Unmodified.* Boston: Harvard University Press, 1987.

————. *Toward a Feminist Theory of State.* Boston: Harvard University Press, 1989.

————. "From Practice to Theory, or What Is a White Woman Anyway?" *Yale Journal of Law and Feminism* 4 (1991): 13–22.

————. "Reflections on Sex Equality under Law." *Yale Law Journal* 100 (1991): 1281–1328.

Mack, Phylis. "Feminine Behavior and Radical Action." In *Rocking the Ship of State,* edited by Yenestra King and Adrienne Harris. London: Westview Press, 1989.

Martin, Emily. *The Woman in the Body: A Cultural Analysis of Reproduction.* Boston: Beacon Press, 1987.

Martin, Gwen. "Selling My Eggs." *Glamour* (May 1994): 168.

Marx, Karl. "Selected Writings." In *The Marx-Engels Reader.* 2nd ed. Edited by Robert C. Tucker. New York: W. W. Norton, 1978.

May, Kathryn. *Back Rooms.* New York: Prometheus Books, 1994.

McElroy, Wendy. "Breeder Reactionaries." *Reason* 26 (1994).

Merchant, Carolyn. *The Death of Nature: Women, Ecology and the Scientific Revolution.* New York: Harper and Row, 1980.

Merrit, Deborah Jones, and Barbara Reskin. "The Hidden Bias of Law Faculties." *Connecticut Law Tribune,* 21 September 1992.

Mies, Maria, and Vandana Shiva. *Ecofeminism.* London: Zed Books, 1993.

Millett, Kate. *Sexual Politics.* New York: Doubleday, 1970.

Minow, Martha, and Elizabeth Spelman. "In Context." *Southern California Law Review* 63 (1990): 1597–652.

Moi, Toril, and Janice Radway, eds. *Materialist Feminism.* Publication of *South Atlantic Quarterly* 93. Durham: Duke University Press, 1994.

Moraga, Cherrie, and Gloria Anzaldúa, eds. *This Bridge Called My Back: Writing by Radical Women of Color.* New York: Kitchen Table, 1983.

Morgan, Robin. *Sisterhood is Powerful.* New York: Random House, 1970.

———. "Feminist Diplomacy." *Ms.* (May/June 1991): 1.

Mueller, Marnie. "Financing High-Tech Reproductive Medical Expenditures." *Stanford Law and Policy Review* 6 (1995): 113–18.

Murphy, Julien. *The Constructed Body: AIDS, Reproductive Technology, and Ethics.* Albany: SUNY Press, 1995.

Murphy, Timothy. "Reproductive Controls and Sexual Destiny." *Bioethics* 4 (1990): 121–42.

Nedelsky, Jennifer. *Private Property and the Limits of American Constitutionalism: The Madisonian Framework and its Legacy.* Chicago: University of Chicago Press, 1990.

Nomination of Ruth Bader Ginsburg to Be an Associate Justice of the United States Supreme Court. Senate Report, serial no. J-103–21 (1993).

Nye, Andrea. *Feminist Theory and the Philosophies of Man.* London: Routledge, 1988.

Nozick, Robert. *Anarchy, State and Utopia.* Oxford: Blackwell, 1968.

Oakley, Ann. *The Captured Womb: A History of Medical Care of Pregnant Women.* Oxford: Basil Blackwell, 1984.

———. *Subject Women.* London: Martin Robertson, 1981.

———. *Women, Medicine and Health.* Edinburgh: Edinburgh University Press, 1993.

O'Brien, Mary. *The Politics of Reproduction.* Boston: Routledge, 1981.

Olsen, Frances. "Constitutional Law: Feminist Critiques of the Public/Private Distinction." *Constitutional Commentary* 10 (1993): 319–27.

Overall, Christine, ed. *The Future of Human Reproduction.* Toronto: Women's Press, 1989.

Pateman, Carole. *The Sexual Contract.* Cambridge: Polity Press, 1988.

Pateman, Carole, and Mary Lyndon Shanley, eds. *Feminist Interpretations and Political Theory.* Cambridge: Polity Press, 1991.

Petchesky, Rosalind Pollack. "Fetal Images: The Power of Visual Culture in the Politics of Reproduction." In *Reproductive Technologies: Gender, Motherhood and Medicine,* edited by Michelle Stanworth. Minneapolis: University of Minnesota Press, 1987.

———. *Abortion and Woman's Choice: The State, Sexuality and Reproductive Freedom.* Boston: Northeastern University Press, 1984.

Pfeffer, Naomi. "Not So New Technologies." *Trouble and Strife* 5 (Spring 1985): 46–50.

———. *The Stork and the Syringe.* Cambridge: Polity Press, 1993.

Phillips, Angela, and Jill Rakusen. *The New Our Bodies, Ourselves: A Health Book by and for Women.* London: Penguin, 1989.

Phillips, Anne, ed. *Feminism and Equality.* New York: New York University Press, 1987.

Piercy, Marge. *Woman on the Edge of Time.* London: The Women's Press, 1978.

Pine, Rachel, and Sylvia Law. "Envisioning a Future for Reproductive Liberty: Strategies for Making Rights Real." *Harvard Civil Rights-Civil Liberties Law Review* 27 (1992): 407–63.

Plant, Judith, ed. *Healing the Wounds: The Promise of Ecofeminism.* Philadelphia: New Society Publishers, 1989.

Pope John Paul II. *Evangelium Vitae.* London: Catholic Truth Society, Publishers to the Holy See, 30 March 1995.

Purdy, Laura. *Reproducing Persons: Issues in Feminist Bioethics.* Ithaca: Cornell University Press, 1996.

Quindlen, Anna. "And Now, Babe Feminism." *The New York Times,* 19 January 1994, editorial page.

Ragoné, Helena. *Surrogate Motherhood: Conception in the Heart.* Oxford: Westview Press, 1994.

Raymond, Janice. "Reproductive Gifts and Gift Giving: The Altruistic Woman." *Hastings Center Report* (November/December 1990): 7–11.

———. *Women as Wombs.* New York: Harper Collins, 1993.

———. "International Traffic in Reproduction." *Ms.* (May/June 1991): 29–32.

Raymond, Janice, Renate Klein, and Lynette Dumble. "RU 486 No." *Ms.* (March/April 1993): 34–37.

Raz, Joseph. *The Morality of Freedom.* Oxford: Clarendon Press, 1986.

Reissman, Catherine Kohler. "Women and Medicalisation: A New Perspective." In *Inventing Women: Science, Technology and Gender,* edited by Gill Kirkup and Laurie Smith Keller. Cambridge: Polity Press, 1992.

Rhode, Deborah, ed. *Theoretical Perspectives on Sexual Difference.* New Haven: Yale University Press, 1990.

Rhoden, Nancy. "The Judge in the Delivery Room: The Emergence of Court-Ordered Cesarean Sections." *California Law Review* 74 (1986): 1951–2030.

———. "Trimesters and Technology: Revamping Roe v. Wade." *Yale Law Journal* 95 (1986): 639–97.

Rich, Adrienne. "Compulsory Heterosexuality and Lesbian Existence." In *The Signs Reader: Women, Gender and Scholarship,* edited by Elizabeth Abel and Emily K. Abel, Chicago: University of Chicago Press, 1983.

———. *Of Woman Born: Motherhood as Experience and Institution.* New York: W.W. Norton, 1976.

Richards, David. "Sexual Autonomy and the Constitutional Right to Privacy: A Case Study in Human Rights and the Unwritten Constitution." *The Hastings Law Journal* (March 1979): 957–1018.

———. *Foundations of American Constitutionalism.* New York: Oxford University Press, 1989.

Ridder, Stephanie, and Lisa Woll. "Transforming the Grounds: Autonomy and Reproductive Freedom." *Yale Journal of Law and Feminism* 2 (1989): 75–98.

Rose, Carol. "Women and Property: Gaining and Losing Ground." *Virginia Law Review* (1992): 209–39.

———. "Bargaining and Gender." *Harvard Journal of Law and Public Policy* 18 (1995): 547–63.

Ross, Loretta. "A Simple Human Right." *On the Issues* (Spring 1994): 22–25.

Rosser, Sue. *Women's Health—Missing From U.S. Medicine.* Bloomington: Indiana University Press, 1994.

Rothman, Barbara Katz. *In Labor: Women and Power in the Birthplace.* London: W.W. Norton, 1982.

———. *Recreating Motherhood: Ideology and Technology in a Patriarchal Society.* New York: W.W. Norton, 1989.

Rowbotham, Sheila. *Woman's Consciousness, Man's World.* New York: Penguin, 1973.

Rowland, Robyn. "Decoding Reprospeak." *Ms.* (May/June 1991): 38–41.

———. *Living Laboratories: Women and Reproductive Technologies.* Bloomington: Indiana University Press, 1992.

Ruddick, Sara. *Maternal Thinking: Toward a Politics of Peace.* New York: Ballantine Books, 1989.

Russ, Joanna. "Recent Feminist Utopias." In *Future Females: A Critical Anthology,* edited by Marleen S. Barr. Bowling Green, OH: Bowling Green State University Popular Press, 1981.

Schafran, Lynn Hecht. "They Just Don't Get It about Rape." *New York Times,* 16 November 1996, editorial page.

Schlafly, Phyllis. *The Power of the Positive Woman.* New York: Arlington House Publishers, 1977.

Schor, Naomi, and Elizabeth Weed, eds. *The Essential Difference.* Bloomington: Indiana University Press, 1994.

Scott, Charity. "Resisting the Temptation to Turn Medical Recommendations into Judicial Orders: A Reconsideration of Court-Ordered Surgery for Pregnant Women." *Georgia State University Law Review* 10 (1994): 615–89.

Scott, Joan. "Cyborgian Socialists?" In *Coming to Terms: Feminism, Theory, Politics,* edited by Elizabeth Weed. New York: Routledge, 1989.

Scutt, Jocelynne, ed. *The Baby Machine: Reproductive Technology and the Commercialisation of Motherhood.* London: Green Print, 1990.

Sen, Gita, and Rachel Snow, eds. *Power and Decision: The Social Control of Reproduction.* Boston: Harvard University Press, 1994.

Shalev, Carmel. *Birth Power.* New Haven: Yale University Press, 1989.

Shultz, Marjorie Maguire. "From Informed Consent to Patient Choice: A New Protected Interest." *Yale Law Journal* 95 (1985): 219–99.

———. "Reproductive Technology and Intent-Based Parenthood: An Opportunity for Gender Neutrality." *University of Wisconsin Law Review* (1990): 290–398.

Siegel, Reva. "Reasoning from the Body." *Stanford Law Review* 44 (1992): 261–381.

Sistare, Christine. "Reproductive Freedom and Women's Freedom: Surrogacy and Autonomy," *Philosophical Forum* 19 (1988): 227–40.

Smith, Barbara, ed. *Home Girls: A Black Feminist Anthology.* New York: Kitchen Table Press, 1983.

Smith, Patricia, ed. *Feminist Jurisprudence*. New York: Oxford University Press, 1993.

Spallone, Patricia. *Beyond Conception: The New Politics of Reproduction*. London: Macmillan, 1989.

Spallone, Patricia and Deborah Lynn Steinberg, eds. *Made to Order: The Myth of Reproductive and Genetic Progress*. Oxford: Pergamon Press, 1987.

Spelman, Elizabeth. *Inessential Woman: Problems of Exclusion in Feminist Thought*. Boston: Beacon Press, 1988.

Stabile, Carol. *Feminism and the Technological Fix*. Manchester: Manchester University Press, 1994.

Staggenborg, Suzanne. *The Pro-Choice Movement: Organization and Activism in the Abortion Conflict*. Oxford: Oxford University Press, 1991.

Stanworth, Michelle. "Birth Pangs: Conceptive Technologies and the Threat to Motherhood." In *Conflicts in Feminism*, edited by Marianne Hirsch and Evelyn Fox Keller. New York: Routledge, 1990.

———, ed. *Reproductive Technologies: Gender, Motherhood, and Medicine*. Cambridge: Polity Press, 1987.

Stone, Deborah. "Fetal Risks, Women's Rights." *The American Prospect* (Fall 1990): 43–53.

Sunstein, Cass, ed. *Feminism and Political Theory*. Chicago: University of Chicago Press, 1990.

Thompson, Judith Jarvis. "A Defense of Abortion." *Philosophy and Public Affairs* (1971): 47–66.

Tong, Rosemarie. *Feminist Thought: A Comprehensive Introduction*. San Francisco: Westview Press, 1989.

Trombley, Stephen. *The Right to Reproduce: A History of Coercive Sterilization*. London: Weindenfeld and Nicolson, 1988.

Tully, Anne [pseud.]. "Working Inside the System." *On the Issues* (Winter 1997): 44–46.

Van Dyck, Jose. *Manufacturing Babies and Public Consent: Debating the New Reproductive Technologies*. London: Macmillan, 1995.

Wajcman, Judy. *Feminism Confronts Technology*. Cambridge: Polity Press, 1991.

Warren, Karen. "Toward an Ecofeminist Ethic." *Studies in the Humanities* (December 1988): 140–56.

Weinbaum, Alys Eve. "Marx, Irigary and the Politics of Representation." *Differences: A Journal of Feminist Cultural Studies* 6 (Spring 1994): 98–128.

Wikler, Norma Juliet. "Society's Response to the New Reproductive Technologies: The Feminist Perspectives." *Southern California Law Review* 59 (1986): 1043–57.

Williams, Joan. "Gender Wars: Selfless Women in the Republic of Choice." *New York University Law Review* 66 (1991): 1559–634.

Williams, Patricia. "Alchemical Notes: Reconstructing Ideals from Deconstructed Rights." *Harvard Civil Rights-Civil Liberties Law Review* 22 (1987): 401–33.

———. "Reflections on Law, Contracts, and the Value of Life." *Ms.* (May/June 1991): 42–46.

Women's Action Coalition (WAC). *WAC Stats: The Facts about Women.* New York: New Press, 1993.

Women's Rights Law Reporter. Fall/Winter 1989.

Young, Iris Marion. *Justice and the Politics of Difference.* Princeton: Princeton University Press, 1990.

INDEX

abortion. *See also* contraception, abortion; activism, 3, 10, 15, 18n8, 58n31, 91–92, 93, 120, 138, 139, 143n23, 144n41; Israel, 7, 116; language of, 65, 102, 103–4, 120, 121; legal right to, 76–79, 81–84, 117, 120, 122–24, 127–135; Medicaid funding for, 62, 83, 87, 120, 151, 155–56; moral right to, 103; parental consent laws, 88, 109n58, 110n62; Romania, 123; sex selection, 63; South Africa, 123; twenty-four hour waiting period, 79
Accreditation Council for Graduate Medical Education (ACGME), 154
Adams, Margaret, 90
African-American women, ix–182
African National Congress (ANC), 123
Allen, Anita, 101, 132, 135
Alpert, Jane, 26, 45
alternative insemination. *See* assisted conception, therapeutic donor insemination
American Association of University Women (AAUW), 71
American Bar Association, 157
American Civil Liberties Union (ACLU), 13
Andrews, Lori, 92
antenatal technology. *See* prenatal technology
Arditti, Rita, 62, 66, 69
assisted conception, 1–5, 11, 63, 81, 85, 87, 93, 136, 137, 139; ancient methods, 11; embryo freezing and transfer, 2, 13, 62, 70, 86, 93, 99, 150; egg

harvesting and donation, 2, 13, 35, 63, 65, 66, 72n4, 85–86, 90, 94, 97, 150, 152; in vitro fertilization (IVF), 2, 12–13, 14, 34, 62, 63, 65, 66, 67, 70, 83, 93, 94, 96, 136, 151; language of, 65, 102, 137; surrogacy, 2, 10, 11, 14, 67, 85–86, 90, 91, 93–97, 99–101, 109n56, 110n67; therapeutic donor insemination (TDI), 2, 13, 14, 18n4, 101, 146n76

Baby M, 85, 88, 100
Barrett, Michéle, 118
Bell, Becky, 88
Bell, Derrick, 157
Benshoof, Janet, 153
Berg, Barbara, 65
Berer, Marge, 68, 71
Biale, Rachel, 6
birth, 1–5, 49–50, 81, 83, 137, 161n4; activism around, 3, 138; anesthesia, 2, 83, 94, 95, 102, 124; Cesarean section, 2, 14, 43, 51, 58n31, 62, 80, 90, 124, 152, 154, 161n3; epidural, 11; episiotomy, 2; forceps, 2, 11–12; home birth, 10; language of, 64–64, 81, 137; maternal mortality, 123, 125; midwifery, 3; natural childbirth, 44, 137, 139; water birth, 3, 10, 151
Bill of Rights, 75
birth control. *See* contraception
Blackmun, Harry, 77, 132
Bradwell v. State, 128
Brandeis, Louis D., 76
Brennan, 129

About the Author

Nancy Lublin was a Marshall Scholar at Oxford University where she earned her M.Litt in Politics before pursuing a law degree at New York University as a Root-Tilden-Snow Scholar. Nancy has spent many years as an abortion-rights and reproductive health activist, most recently working on issues surrounding childbirth. She is currently the executive director of Dress for Success New York, a service providing professional clothing to low-income women pursuing employment. Ms. magazine recently honored her as one of "21 young feminists to watch in the 21st century."

New Feminist Perspectives Series
General Editor: Rosemarie Tong, Davidson College